VODOU
Money Magic

"Vodou Money Magic is like a car jack: if you aren't afraid to get your hands dirty, it will help you get the job done. The author explains what steps to take, but you have to do the work yourself."

ELIZABETH BARRETTE, AUTHOR OF *COMPOSING MAGIC: HOW TO CREATE MAGICAL SPELLS, RITUALS, BLESSINGS, CHANTS AND PRAYER*

VODOU
Money Magic

The Way to Prosperity through the Blessings of the Lwa

Kenaz Filan

Destiny Books

Rochester, Vermont • Toronto, Canada

Destiny Books
One Park Street
Rochester, Vermont 05767
www.DestinyBooks.com

Destiny Books is a division of Inner Traditions International

Library of Congress Cataloging-in-Publication Data

Filan, Kenaz.
  Vodou money magic : the way to prosperity through the blessings of the lwa / Kenaz Filan.
      p. cm.
  Includes bibliographical references and index.
  Summary: "A working guide on how to achieve financial success by working with the lwa, the spirits of Haitian Vodou"—Provided by publisher.
  ISBN 978-1-59477-331-0
  1. Voodooism—Haiti. 2. Haiti—Religion. 3. Money—Miscellanea. 4. Magic. I. Title.
  BL2530.H3F56 2010
  299.6'75173—dc22

2009040423

Printed and bound in The United States by Lake Book Manufacturing, Inc.

10   9   8   7   6   5   4   3   2   1

Text design and layout by Virginia Scott Bowman
This book was typeset in Garamond Premier Pro with Abbess, Avenir, and Futura as display typefaces

To send correspondence to the author of this book, mail a first-class letter to the author c/o Inner Traditions • Destiny Books, One Park Street, Rochester, VT 05767, and we will forward the communication.

Contents

Preface

ACCORDING TO SOME, GETTING rich is the simplest thing in the world. One need only visualize prosperity, chant abundance mantras, or join the right multilevel marketing plan and soon the money will be flowing in. Keys to wealth are as thick on the ground as ultimate weight-loss guides.

For most Haitians, prosperity means having enough to eat; wealth is a little bit of money stashed away against the inevitable hard times. Pipe dreams and get-rich-quick schemes are a luxury they can ill afford. They know that every triumph demands sacrifice, that behind every success are a dozen failures. For almost three hundred years they have relied on Vodou to give them an edge in one of the Western Hemisphere's harshest environments.

Cynics frequently ask, "If Vodou is so powerful, why is Haiti the poorest country in the Western Hemisphere?" We might turn the question around. Vodou has survived a century of slavery, three centuries of oppression, nineteen years of U.S. occupation of Haiti, and innumerable efforts by state and church (Evangelical and Catholic) to eradicate this "primitive superstition." Like the Haitian people, Vodou exists in the face of overwhelming odds; its continued existence is testimony to its power and to the strength of its followers.

Many modern magicians have internalized a cultural disdain for money. Most strains of British traditional witchcraft explicitly prohibit charging for initiations. Many Neopagans go further and forbid charging a client for any magical or spiritual services; some would even condemn using magic to improve one's personal finances. (It can lead to selfishness and materialism, you know.) And not surprisingly, many of these people who scorn wealth discover that wealth scorns them back.

Yet historically, magic has long been a tool for gain. People once went to witches to seek prosperity and success, not spiritual folderol and soothing words. Magicians were judged by their miracles and paid for their skill in producing them. In Haiti, Vodou is not just a religion; it is also a career opportunity. A gift for working with the *lwa* (spirits) and satisfying a clientele has made some houngans and mambos wealthy and has kept many others in relative prosperity in one of the world's poorest countries.

In Cap-Haïtien, Haiti's second-largest city, Mayor Michel St. Croix estimates that less than 10 percent of the city's eight hundred thousand residents have jobs. Thanks to aid from the international community, St. Croix was able to provide four hundred street-cleaning jobs that each paid three dollars a day—a sizable wage in a country where 76 percent of the population lives on less than two dollars a day.[1]

If we wish to learn about wealth magic, we may want to explore how *Vodouisants*—practitioners of Vodou—have found prospects for advancement in a place where opportunity is in desperately short supply. A great part of a tradition's magic lies in its way of seeing; there is more power in wisdom than in spell craft. Teaching the ins and outs of Vodou practice lies beyond the scope of this book (or indeed any book, series, or website). Learning the preconceptions and prejudices of the Vodou worldview—and of our own—may prove more useful.

The Blessings of Poverty, the Blessings of Wealth

Romanticism gave us "states of Nature" and pre-Christian utopias untouched by the taint of civilization. The Romantics followed the lead of Jean-Jacques Rousseau, who honored "man in his primitive state, as he is placed by nature at an equal distance from the stupidity of brutes, and the fatal ingenuity of civilized man."[2] Many Romantic philosophers equated wealth with civilization and all its attendant evils. As Henry David Thoreau wrote:

> If you are restricted in your range by poverty, if you cannot buy books and newspapers, for instance, you are but confined to the most significant and vital experiences; you are compelled to deal with the material which yields the most sugar and the most starch. It is life near the bone where it is sweetest . . . Superfluous wealth can buy superfluities only. Money is not required to buy one necessity of the soul.[3]

A Marxist/Luddite distaste for business was combined later with Eastern asceticism as Theosophy, Vedantism, and other movements brought Buddhist and Hindu ideas of renunciation to Victorian and Edwardian occulture. Since these movements were largely the provenance of the moneyed classes, there was an accompanying disdain for too-obvious ambition. Wealth magic was low sorcery: it showed greed and, worse, that the magician needed money.

Whereas Victorian magicians had mixed feelings about wealth, the mid-twentieth-century counterculture had open hostility toward it. In 1970 England's Isle of Wight Festival degenerated into a battle between promoters and radicals bemoaning entertainment for profit and demanding a free event. "[I]t began as a beautiful dream but it has gotten out of control and become a monster," said promoter Ron Foulk in his epitaph for what would prove to be the last festival on Wight for thirty-two years.[4] In America the Summer of Love was replaced by several long, hot summers of rioting against "The Establishment" and contempt for the faceless gray bourgeoisie. Financial success was a sign of moral turpitude; "working-class cred" was superior to inherited (or even hard-earned) wealth.

By contrast, Haitian Vodouisants know that poverty doesn't make most people saintly or blessed, it just makes them poor. To renounce worldly goods you must first have them, and fasting is only a virtue when it is voluntary. In Vodou, poverty is a sign of weakness; good fortune is a sign that one is favored by *Bondye* (God) and the *lwa* (spirits). Vodouisants seek not to accept their condition but to rise above it. In an intensely competitive environment, they believe Vodou provides an edge that can make the difference between hope and despair, between survival and death.

A lack of resources and an overabundance of people ensure that very little is free in Haiti. This is reflected in Vodou's religious and magical worldview. The lwa expect to be paid for their favors and Vodouisants expect to be rewarded—by both their clients and the spirits—for their services. Vodouisants have no compunction about demanding money from the lwa or withholding their offerings if they don't get a response. There are clearly delineated expectations that priest, client, and lwa are expected to meet, with little room for excuses on any part.

To survive amid scarcity requires a community. The *famni* (family) shares resources and closes ranks against outside dangers. In exchange for the family's protection, the individual pledges loyalty and service to the group. This is true of spiritual relations as well as blood ties (the two oft being entwined in Haiti): the *société* (Vodou house) looks after its members, and functions as a support group as well as a religious organization. A similar dynamic holds for the interaction between lwa and servitor. The lwa give special attention to those who give them special attention and tangible rewards to those who make tangible offerings. It is a relationship of mutual need and mutual respect.

If neglected, the lwa may take away the Vodouisant's wealth and luck. Conversely, servitors may withhold service from their lwa after a period of misfortune or signs that the spirits have been slacking on their end. This may seem disrespectful, but it's in keeping with tradition. Practitioners of Goetic magic (strains of which have influenced many sociétés in Haiti) coerce demons to do their bidding through negative reinforcement, and J. G. (Sir James George) Frazer (1854–1941) described how Sicilian Catholics in 1893 responded to a prolonged drought by putting their saints outside and taking away their ornaments until they brought rain.[5] Ultimately, it comes down to economics: in Haiti even a lwa who will not work will not eat.

Vodou, Poverty, and Practicality

This may seem harsh, even mercenary, to those of us raised in more indulgent faiths. We may prefer that our gods shower blessings upon us in exchange for nothing more than a sincere "thank you." And while we may have no compunction about asking for "strength," for "the best possible outcome," or for other equally nebulous requests, we might agonize for a long time before petitioning our gods for a new car or a raise at work. "Do I really *need* this?" we might ask. "Will it be useful to my spiritual development?" But are we worried that the gods might be offended by our greed—or afraid that they may not be able to deliver our requests?

Although scorned as "primitive superstition," Vodou is actually a very practical and scientific tradition. The petitions that are offered to the lwa are tangible and easily verified: In the words of the Viennese school of logical positivists, they are "falsifiable." It is difficult to say whether a ritual aimed at granting "inner peace" is a failure or a success. By contrast, a successful money *wanga* (magic spell) will show definite and verifiable results: one's financial situation either improves or does not improve.

Many modern "magicians" enjoy the aesthetics of magic; they find the practice of ritual stimulating and therapeutic. Few regularly put themselves in situations where they must live or die by their magic. Haitian Vodouisants, on the other hand, can allow themselves no such luxury. For them magic means the difference between dying and surviving, between surviving and thriving. In this harsh arena, only the most faithful and hardworking spirits will receive regular service; only the most effective wangas and techniques will become part of the Vodouisant's magical arsenal. These spells have worked for centuries in a harsh and impoverished environment; they can certainly yield results amid our more prosperous surroundings.

There are no get-rich-quick schemes and no easy money to be found here. Vodouisants know that the path to wealth is rarely quick and never easy. There are no genies waiting to fulfill your every desire. Vodou can offer you allies; it can introduce you to the lwa and help you to start a mutually beneficial relationship. What happens after that is entirely between you and your spirits.

So what are we waiting for? Let's get down to business.

So What Is This "Vodou" Stuff, Anyway—and Why the Funny Spelling?

THAT'S AN EXCELLENT QUESTION, even if it is a rhetorical one. Political wonks may remember George Bush Sr. scornfully referring to Ronald Reagan's budgetary proposals as "voodoo economics." You may even have stuck a few pins in a "voodoo doll" while wishing the worst for some enemy. (Contrary to popular belief, voodoo dolls are not well known in Haiti. The practice of creating "poppets"—figurines of wax or cloth—and using them for sympathetic magic comes from European witchcraft, not African or Caribbean traditions.) For some the word *voodoo* has an air of sinister magic; for others, a taint of silly superstition.

Vodou, by contrast, is a term for the magico-religious practices of Haiti, a country located on the western half of Hispaniola, an island in the Caribbean. (The eastern side of the island is the Dominican Republic.) "Vodou" is the spelling most commonly used in Kreyol, the language of the Haitian people. This spelling distinguishes it from its primary ancestor, the "Vodun," or "Vodu," practiced in modern-day Benin and Togo by Africans whose ancestors were fortunate enough to escape the slavers. It also distinguishes Vodou from New Orleans voodoo, folk practices that show the influence of Haitian slaves brought to Louisiana by colonists escaping the Saint-Domingue uprising (1791–1804).

Vodou's cosmology is monotheistic and deistic. After creating the world, Bondye (God) withdrew from it. One might pray to Bondye on Sundays at church, but you would hardly expect Him to help you with your personal problems. Instead, you would call on the *lwa*—the spirits that Bondye charged with the day-to-day running of things. Just as the Catholic saints and angels are tasked with keeping things in order, as are the ancestors, so too are a number of Haitian and African entities who are known to their devotees as the lwa.

The lwa are honored at *fets,* parties that feature drumming, dancing, and often the ritual sacrifice of one or more animals. In Haiti these fets are often held in the *peristyle,* a temple owned by the société (Vodou house); in the United States they are sometimes held in the homes of devotees. These fets feature tables filled with offerings for the various lwa who will be saluted. Mama Danto will have a plate full of her favorite dish, *griot* (fried pork). Zaka's bag of food and tools will be found there, as will Agwe's boat and Damballah's egg and flour. On the floor you will find *vévés,* elaborate cornmeal drawings that are used to call down the spirits.

During those fets, the lwa will frequently come down and possess one or more of the attendees. Things are kept in order by a *houngan* (priest) or *mambo* (priestess) who has been initiated in the *kanzo,* a lengthy, grueling ceremony that culminates when the participants receive the *asson,* an elaborately beaded rattle. The asson is both a sign of office and a tool that can be used to call on the spirits and induce possession. The lwa are saluted with the asson and with ceremonial gestures taught to those who are members of the house.

Houngans and mambos can also call down the spirits privately when they need to work wanga (magic) for themselves or a client. This may involve something as simple as burning a candle or it may be a complex ritual involving expensive offerings and hours of prayers and chants. For most Vodou professionals, this is their primary source of income. People call on them to act as intercessors with the lwa; they believe that the Vodouisants' training and affiliation mean that their petitions will receive closer scrutiny. (Corporations and special-interest groups hire lobbyists for the same reason and at a considerably higher price.)

Vodou is an initiatory tradition: to become a houngan or mambo, one must receive training and undergo an initiatory ceremony from a properly made priest or priestess. However, one does not have to be an initiate to serve the lwa or to reap the benefits of working with them. Indeed, most Haitian Vodouisants are not initiated. What is important is developing a personal relationship with your lwa.

You cannot (and should not!) do possession work on your own. Neither should you try holding a large public party for the spirits, or setting yourself up in business as a houngan or mambo without the proper training and initiation. However, there is no reason why you cannot talk to the lwa and ask for their advice and assistance in your daily life. This book will introduce you to some of the most well known and beloved of the lwa, and provide you with some spells that you can use to improve your condition. It is up to you to make that connection—only you can establish that relationship and make these spirits your counselors, guides, and friends.

PART ONE

＊

Worldviews

TO PRACTICE VODOU EFFECTIVELY, we need to learn how to think like Vodouisants. To do this, we first need to understand how their attitudes and preconceptions differ from our own. Effective money magic is more than cryptic words and gestures; it involves overcoming our negative, dysfunctional behaviors and ideas. We may wish to follow a sanitized, whitewashed version of Vodou that lets us do the spells while holding onto all of our cherished ethical tenets and soothing myths. But we will have more success if we explore Vodou honestly, taking it not as we wish it were but, instead, as it is. In doing so, we may find ourselves faced with some important, if uncomfortable, questions about our own lives and ideals.

1
Power

Nearly all men can stand adversity, but if you want to test a man's character, give him power.

ABRAHAM LINCOLN

VODOU IS NOT ABOUT finding enlightenment or attaining inner peace. Vodou is about power. Vodouisants practice their religion so they can gain mastery over their peers and their environment. They work with the spirits to gain that mastery; should the lwa withhold their boons, their followers will not hesitate to withhold offerings. This may seem harsh, even mercenary, to those who come to Vodou as outsiders. We might prefer a world in which we offer our deities the same unconditional love they shower upon us, where even the "dark" gods are only there to teach us valuable life lessons. But if we are to understand Vodou as it is, rather than as we might like it to be, we must explore the rules and preconceptions of its moral universe—and of our own.

Power as a Five-Letter Word

Our relationship with power is ambivalent at best. From an early age we are warned that power corrupts. We're expected to confine our quest to power over self (typically meaning self-denial and self-abnegation) and cautioned against the black magic of power over others. We are taught to shun those who obviously wish to rise beyond their social station and

7

become leaders; if they aren't considered "sell-outs," they are deemed "power hungry" and hence are not to be trusted. We're taught to hold sacred tenets of democracy and egalitarianism. Claims that we are better than someone else are to be made in extreme moderation, lest we be accused of bragging or groveling.

In our culture, raw displays of power are distasteful because they are unnecessary. The population can be pacified by all the baubles of a consumer culture; there is plenty to go around. We can have laborers who fancy themselves members of the middle class, complete with mortgage, car payment, and wide-screen HDTV. This is not and has never been the case in Haiti. There are no circuses and very little bread. The scarce resources are largely controlled by a wealthy elite who rule through intimidation and terror. A "neg" (literally, "black"; a more accurate translation might be "poor man") has no illusions that he was created equal to his rulers. Should these rulers wish, they can evict him from his ancestral land; they can jail him for any reason or no reason; they can kill him should he prove a threat or even an annoyance. His very existence (and that of his fellow have-nots, who make up 80 percent of Haiti's population) is at the sufferance of the ruling elite.

Produced under this yoke, you might expect Vodou's theology to demonize the arrogant mighty and extol the virtues of poverty and humility. Instead, Vodou practitioners have developed a keen respect for power and have learned to cherish every scrap of it that they might acquire. Vodou sees no particular nobility in poverty, no special holiness in being a victim; those "blessings" are freely available throughout Haiti. On the contrary, those whom the lwa favor they bless with prosperity and success. Power is not an invitation to divine chastisement but a sign of divine favor.

Vodouisants may hate those who oppress them. They may wreak a terrible vengeance when given a chance, as in the bloody *dechoukage* (uprootings) that claimed hundreds of lives after coups in 1986, 1988, and 1991.[1] But there is always a certain conviction that this oppression is preordained, an expectation—generally fulfilled—that the new leaders will be no better than the old; that "Behind the mountains are mountains and more mountains";[2] and that "when neg fights neg, God laughs." There is no idea that everything happens "for the greater good" or that there is some heavenly reward at the end. The wealthy may assuage their consciences by thinking of the celestial prizes awaiting the less fortunate, but the poor are not so naive. Three hundred years of Haitian history have given them little reason to expect a better tomorrow, either here or in the hereafter.

Power, Power Exchange, and the Spirits

Many of our ideas about divine rule and heavenly order come from a prosperous Christian bishop named St. Augustine of Hippo (354–430 CE). His vision, as portrayed in his book *City of God,* was inspired largely by the social and political structures of the late Roman Empire. Later we incorporated ideas from Hinduism and Buddhism as filtered through a ruling-class Victorian English mindset. To these people the universe was a logical and well-mannered place; their privileged status was proof of heaven's benevolence and willingness to grant gifts to the deserving. To the extent that all of human history and all of human culture culminated in their ruling-class Victorian English society, so all other stories of the divine were but shadows of their God or reflections of their Truth.

Vodou, by contrast, arose out of the horrors of the Middle Passage, the middle leg of a trade triangle in which slaves were transported from Africa to the Americas via Europe. These earliest adherents of Vodou were yanked from their homes and taken to strange places on the other side of the world, where they were worked mercilessly on plantations and subjected to savage punishments for the slightest disobedience. Their theology had no place for a kindly divinity showering blessings on his people. Bondye, Vodou's vision of God, is not so much a benevolent emperor as an absentee ruler, as inapproachable as the *gran blancs* who owned the plantations and simultaneously as vital and unimportant in their daily lives. That is still true today; now, although Bondye may be given a verbal nod in prayers or through attendance at Sunday Mass, He generally keeps his distance from the affairs of men—and certainly from the affairs of poor Haitians.

Rather than concern themselves with the inaccessible and inscrutable Bondye, Vodouisants focus on the spirits who work under Him and who are responsible for overseeing His affairs. Like most bureaucrats, the lwa are inclined to look favorably upon petitions from those Vodouisants they already know, or in Vodou parlance, those they "walk with." Others will require an introduction through a mutual acquaintance; one of the main reasons for joining a société is to gain access to their spirits. And in keeping with the traditional mores of Haitian bureaucracy, these lwa expect flattery and bribes in exchange for their efforts. Some are more benevolent and generously disposed while others will be more demanding and less tolerant of failures; none are inclined to offer unconditional gifts.

One of the few ways in which a poor Haitian can gain status is through Vodou. Membership in a société means protection and better access to scarce opportunities; initiation as a houngan or mambo confers status akin to a law or medical degree. The spirits grant power to those they favor, and Vodou is the science of making them well disposed on your behalf. Many Vodouisants act not out of reverence or love for the lwa but for career advancement; still others are forced into service by ancestral spirits claiming a debt. A *djab* (untamed spirit) who helped your great-grandmother may recruit you into the family tradition, two generations of Evangelicalism notwithstanding. The idea that the divine must gain your consent before taking control of your life is foreign to Haitian Vodou.

But the relationship between Vodouisant and lwa is not just one of bondage and fawning submission. If Vodouisants are *serviteurs lwa* (servants of the spirits), they are servants under contract who will not hesitate to assert their rights and make demands. Vodouisants who have one or more powerful spirits will be able to earn a living performing wanga for others. As their reputation grows, they may be able to afford more impressive quarters for their lwa. They might be able to purchase initiation and gain those social and magical benefits. They will gain followers of their own who will come to the spirit with offerings and sacrifices. Each hand washes the other, and each party in the spiritual transaction has expectations that must be fulfilled. In a land with endemic scarcity of resources, not even the saints and angels can expect a free lunch.

Vodou and Power over Others

Most of us have come of age in a culture that granted us considerable leeway to state our opinions. We may have participated in college protests or written impassioned letters to our local newspapers. We may have worn T-shirts condemning our political leaders in strong or even scatological terms, or even flaunted our membership in one or more alternative cultures and reveled in shocking the mundanes. We take these freedoms as a birthright and consider them the hallmark of a civilized culture. We would (and regularly do) condemn any government that enforces restrictions in dress, speech, or lifestyle. We certainly have no use for a person or party who would hijack someone else's emotions and take control of another's "free will."

Haitian Vodouisants live in a very different world. The Haitian rulers are well aware that they preside over an unstable situation: between 1804 and 2005, Haiti experienced thirty-two coups. A Haitian politician who tolerates an actual or perceived challenge to his position may lose that position. Vodouisants who speak out on behalf of one side may be killed by the other side; drawing the attention of the powerful is more likely to bring trouble than benefit. The daily existence of most poor Haitians shows little evidence of free will; rather, they are constantly reminded of their restrictions and limitations. As a result, we can hardly be surprised that Vodou has never developed taboos against controlling or doing harm to others.

Haiti is a dangerous place; Haitians have learned to take precautions against those dangers. There is an expectation that others will show similar forethought, and there is little sympathy for those who do not. Childhood stories describe the adventures of Ti Malis, a clever thief and trickster who regularly takes advantage of his well-meaning but dull-witted "friend" Ti Bouki. The implied moral of these stories is that it is better to be smart like Ti Malis than trusting like Ti Bouki.[3] Most interactions between strangers are marked by mutual mistrust and suspicion; fear of poisoning and sorcery is widespread. (Indeed, many Haitians joke that there is no such thing as death by natural causes in Haiti, since any demise will be greeted with speculation about jealous neighbors.)

Vodou does not condemn coercive or destructive magic, but neither does it doubt its existence. Haitian Vodouisants know that others may resort to wanga and take appropriate steps to defend themselves. Initiation is said to confer immunity to many forms of malevolent magic, while a *gad migan* (stomach guard) is believed to neutralize spiritual and physical poisons. But the Vodouisant's greatest protection against all of these is a solid working relationship with his spirits. If the lwa are happy, they will deflect many difficulties, defuse most magical threats, and provide the tools necessary to overcome others in the fiercely competitive struggle for survival.

Vodou, Power, and the Family

This is not to say that Vodou is without ethics or that poor Haitians have no moral code. But those ethics are largely focused on the société and its members; that moral code is geared almost exclusively toward the individual's immediate family. One's primary duty is to ones blood relatives. In Haitian culture to call someone *sanmaman*—"without a mother"—is a grievous insult, as it implies that the person is so worthless that even his or her own family has cast him or her out. In our culture, on the other hand, we like to think that we can rise above our origins and create ourselves in our own image. But Haitian Vodouisants define and are defined by their roots; for them, ancestry is both identity and destiny.

Family relationships are so valued because they can be the difference between life and death. Multiple children mean more mouths to feed—but they also mean more potential workers to bring in money for rice, beans, and other staples. A tightknit family that cares for its members and shares its wealth in good times can better weather bad times. A lone individual may be robbed or killed with impunity; connections to powerful people or membership in a well-regarded Vodou house (or a feared secret society such as the Sanpwel) can provide much-needed protection. Hence, these relationships are cherished and the attendant responsibilities emphasized.

Vodou, Power, and Race

Discussions of class and privilege make many of us uncomfortable; talk of racial issues sends us into a frothing rage. According to some, racism no longer exists. Others will tell you that little has changed since the days of Martin Luther King and Malcolm X, and that we're still living under de facto apartheid. Conversations about race frequently devolve into shouting matches that shed much heat but little light. We talk constantly of racism, yet seem incapable of holding a reasoned discussion on the topic.

With the advent of affirmative action and similar programs, race (and other categories such as sexual orientation, gender, religion, and disability status) has become its own sort of power. Being a member of a minority group can now offer access to scholarships, preferences in hiring and business, and legal protections. This has led some nonminorities to complain of the affront to our myth of equality. It has led others to emphasize their membership in one or more minority groups to claim their slice of the victim pie and absolve themselves of the sin of privilege.

The question of race is at least as important in Haiti as it is in the

United States. Much of Haitian history has revolved around conflict between the light-skinned, French-speaking, wealthy "milats" (mulattos) and the darker-skinned, Kreyol-speaking, poor negs. But while a few leaders (notably François Duvalier and Jean-Bertrand Aristide) have come to power by appealing to Haiti's poor blacks, there has never been anything like our "Black is beautiful" movement. As a result, rich and poor alike openly favor light skin over dark skin and consider French superior to Kreyol.

Haitians are quick to recognize putting on airs. One proverb states, *"Pal franse pa di lespri pou sa,"* or, "Speaking French doesn't mean you are smart." They also realize that money trumps race; as yet another proverb puts it, *"Milat pov se neg, neg rich se milat,"* or, "A poor mulatto is black, a wealthy black is mulatto."[4] Affecting the mannerisms of wealth is one thing; having the actual wherewithal is quite another. The trappings of milat culture are desirable because they give the appearance of power—but Haitians know very well that appearances can be deceiving. Skin color may be an obstacle but it is not an utterly insurmountable one; by the same token, neither is it a guarantee of privilege.

These open prejudices can be very off-putting, even painful, to African Americans. While questions of skin privilege have long been important within the African American community, they have typically simmered beneath the surface. Longstanding fears of miscegenation and "race-mixing" led to the Jim Crow era's "one drop" benchmark. By that standard, one drop of African blood made you "colored." A light-skinned black person who could not or did not wish to "pass" as white could expect little in the way of special treatment from Caucasian society. White people saw race issues in terms of black and white; nuances of complexion, hair, and features were of interest mostly to those of African descent.

Indeed, we might like all these thorny issues to untangle themselves amid the warm glow of universal brotherhood and fellowship. Failing that, we might wish to hide them beneath a blanket of silence. Our generation has come to equate racism with the use of racially derogatory language; actions and attitudes are given far less weight than utterances about race.

Haitian Vodou does not allow us that luxury. It is a mirror that reflects both our beauty and our flaws: in condemning the lwa, we condemn ourselves.

Vodou, Power, and Danger

Many modern-day magicians loudly boast that they are as harmless as declawed kittens. Many New Age paradigms claim that their teachings can only be used for the highest and greatest good, and that since they come from the realms of Spirit, they of course should only be used for positive ends. Whereas witches were once accused of blighting crops and murdering infants, today some will tell you that no true witch would ever work to harm another. Much of the false accusation comes from one of modern occcultism's most enduring legends, the "Burning Times." These tales of millions of murdered witches have long been proven inaccurate. Historians estimate that forty thousand people were executed, most of those vagrants, heretic Christians, and other unfortunates.[5] Still, the idea of impending slaughter has become deeply ingrained. Hence, many seek to present their religion as safe and nonthreatening in hopes that this will promote acceptance and prevent future pogroms.

Most Vodouisants, by contrast, are happy to cultivate an ominous image. A mambo whose spirits will not harm his (or his clients') enemies would soon be seeking another line of work. The secret societies make little effort to debunk accusations of corpse-eating, zombification, and human sacrifice. Persecution is an integral part of Vodou's history; hence, Vodouisants have learned firsthand the folly of proclaiming oneself defenseless. They know that lynch mobs are more easily dissuaded by fear of retribution than by claims of benevolence. A sorcerer who is rumored to be in league with Le Roi Lecife (King Lucifer) or a powerful djab may be the target of neighborhood gossip, but he or she is not likely to be the target of robbers or kidnappers.

For many of us, it is more important to be liked than to be feared; indeed, we may even think the two are mutually exclusive. We want to reassure everyone who might be intimidated by us that we mean them no harm, that we only have their best interests at heart. If we show our strength we may scare away potential clients or offend our superiors; if we defend ourselves, we may be perceived as uncooperative or even hostile. By working with the stern but nurturing warrior mother Ezili Danto (see chapter 13), we can learn how to be both strong and caring—a skill that will serve us well in both our business and personal lives. Meditating on Ogou and his mysteries (see chapter 12) can give us the courage to express our power when we need to.

Note well that being feared has nothing to do with affecting a spooky appearance or threatening all and sundry with your dark Satanic curses. Most of the symbols we associate with black magic are drawn from horror films: they are theatrical and hence carry with them the advertisement for their falsehood. At best, they make you look like someone playacting a role; at worst they suggest you are incapable of distinguishing between fantasy and reality. This does not inspire the fear that breeds respect but rather the dread that sane people feel in the presence of the delusional.

The best houngans and mambos don't need to brag about their sinister connections or their mighty magical abilities. The reputation they have earned is all the advertising they need. The friends and family members they have helped—and the enemies who have felt their vengeance—speak for them. They use both their community's love and fear to their best advantage: they recognize that both are vital tools in preserving their status and both are an integral part of power. It is a lesson that those seeking success (in other words, all of us) would do well to learn.

Vodou, Power, and Trust

Many of us would agree with Will Rogers that "A stranger is just a friend I haven't met yet." We live in a world where we can get away with such a belief. In Haiti, however, a stranger may be your death. Kidnappings are an everyday occurrence, touching the lives of Haiti's rich and poor alike, and law enforcement has been largely indifferent if not complicit. Gang violence and gunfire are commonplace; those people you don't know may well be *kriminels* (assassins) or *voleurs* (thieves). They may have powerful enemies—or powerful friends. A hand foolishly extended in friendship may be as dangerous as a rash blow.

As a result, Haitians generally greet strangers with neutrality and a good deal of suspicion. Newcomers are apprised first as potential threats. Once it is established that they are not an immediate threat, the next questions arise: Who are you? Where are you from? Why are you here? What do you want? The *temwen* (testimony) of friends and relatives will be used to determine character, through the ever-popular *teledjol* (tele-jawbone, or gossip). A neighbor's friend in Vieux Carre may know the stranger's mother; before long, everyone in town will be familiar with stories of the stranger's childhood. One who does not have that temwen will find it very difficult to melt that cool reserve.

This is not to say that one without connections cannot become a member of the community. As we have already seen, the asson lineage became popular largely because it offered new spiritual and social ties to uprooted migrants. For our purposes the important lesson is this: trust is not given but earned, and at considerable cost. Poor Haitians may save for years to become initiated or to hold public ceremonies for their lwa. While the spiritual dimension is important to them, so too is the social recognition they confer; both are means of gaining power. (Indeed, this helps keep the handshakes, passwords, and other oathbound material secret; to share it would be to devalue one's investment.)

If we are to be more successful, perhaps we should emulate this approach to strangers and new situations. All too often we extend our trust to all who ask, until they prove themselves unworthy. A measured politeness and quiet distance might be a better first response. We are defined by our acquaintances at least as much as by our clothes. Perhaps we should be as selective with our friends as with our wardrobe.

We might also do well to ask ourselves, in our social and business dealings, "What do they want from me?" Unconditional love generally isn't; the same goes for free lunches. By the same token, ask "What do they have to offer me?" If you ask these questions about all of the people in your life, you may be surprised to find that many are taking more than they give. In that case, you may or may not want to consider limiting them or cutting them off. You may benefit from applying that polite, noncommittal Haitian neutrality when dealing with those who would take advantage of your good nature, and saving your resources for people who deserve your attention.

Suppose you showed loyalty to those peers who had earned your loyalty—and cut off those who weren't there for you in time of need. Recognize that friendship is power shared, not power given. A relationship that does not meet your needs might be more aptly described as a donation on your part. Your time and your emotional resources are valuable; as such, they should be treated with respect and not given away lightly. You might not need to assume that everyone is a threat out to destroy you—but there's certainly no reason to assume that everyone loves you unconditionally, either!

Vodou, Power, and You

This raw celebration of greed and ambition may seem disconcerting. You might prefer to wrap yourself in the warm mantle of moral superiority over this sad state of affairs. It's tempting to blame racism, imperialism, and the ruling classes—especially since it lets *us* off the hook! We might instead explore the ways in which power plays out in our lives. Vodouisants cling desperately to their power because it is all they have. In the end, your power is all that *you* have. You will do well to understand that and act accordingly.

2
Entitlement

We hold these truths to be self-evident, that all men are
created equal, that they are endowed by their Creator
with certain unalienable Rights, that among these are
Life, Liberty, and the pursuit of Happiness.

THE DECLARATION OF INDEPENDENCE, 1776

MANY OF AMERICA'S FOUNDING myths rest on the concept of the "inalienable rights of man." A cursory glance of American history will show that these ideals have not always been put into practice. Thomas Jefferson, author of the Declaration of Independence, was also a slaveholder; if he believed his field hands and house servants had been created equal, his actions did little to show it. "Enemy combatants" held at Guantanamo Bay and other secret prisons would be thrilled to learn that they have a right to liberty. The Confederate states that exercised their right to institute new government discovered that inalienable rights were no match for superior firepower. And only the most naive would claim that someone with the capital to hire a crack legal team is not at an advantage over an impoverished defendant who must rely on an overworked public defender.

Nevertheless, the idea of "inalienable rights" has become an integral part of the American psyche. We have extended those rights of "life, liberty, and the pursuit of happiness" to include the right to say and do whatever we want, whenever we want, with no fear of consequences, so long as nobody gets hurt. Instead of a right to "the pursuit of happiness," we have come to believe that we have a right to happiness itself. The dream of a better life has become an expectation: we demand annual raises and steady improvement in our financial and social conditions, and protest loudly when we don't receive them.

Indeed, those born after 1970 have come to be known as "The Entitlement Generation." From an early age they have received positive affirmation from parents, teachers, and coaches; like the children of Garrison Kieler's Lake Wobegon, they were all above average. Raised on a steady diet of instant messages and instant gratification, they have little patience for starting at the bottom and working their way up. They expect that their employers and clients will recognize their genius and immediately place them in high-paying jobs. But all too often, they find themselves disappointed as they enter the land where not everyone gets a gold star for trying.

There is certainly something to be said for self-assurance. Coming to a job interview with an attitude of "I can do this and I will get this job" is certainly more productive than shuffling in with an air of "Oh God, let's get this over with so they can reject me like the other fifty companies did." But there is a fine line between self-confidence and overconfidence, or arrogance. Remember that the words "prima donna" were originally used to designate the leading lady in an opera company. You can get away with behaving like a diva if you have the talent to back up your cocky demeanor. Otherwise, you're likely to be shown the stage door.

If you hope to succeed in magic—or in anything else—you will need to overcome the idea that the world (or any part thereof) owes you something. Meditate upon the wisdom of science fiction writer Robert A. Heinlein, who taught us TANSTAAFL (There Ain't No Such Thing as a Free Lunch). Remember that anything you are given can also be taken away. And, since you came here to learn about Vodou money magic, consider the worldview of the typical Haitian Vodouisant.

Entitlement in Haiti

In Haiti approximately 45 percent of the country's wealth is owned by 1 percent of the population; 80 percent of its population lives in brutal poverty and struggles to survive on less than two dollars a day. Malnutrition is widespread; after the hurricanes of 2008, many of the poor resorted to eating mud cakes to ease their ever-present hunger pangs. These statistics and anecdotes are familiar to anyone who has ever studied Haiti—but what do they really mean?

While Port-au-Prince's poor struggle against hunger and violence in Bel Air and Cité Soleil, its privileged class can be found atop the steep mountains in the suburb of Pétionville. Named after mulatto leader and Haitian president Alexandre Pétion (1770–1818), Pétionville is the richest neighborhood in Haiti. Among its residents are Haiti's business elite, international reporters on assignment, foreign diplomats, and others; its streets are home to high-end shops, art galleries, upscale hotels, and trendy clubs.

Pétionville has also long been one of Haiti's safest neighborhoods. Its residents enjoy friendly relations with the Haitian National Police and have the capital to pay former soldiers and other security forces to patrol their streets and protect them from the gangs that terrorize Port-au-Prince's less fortunate. In keeping with Haitian history, the military and police exist to protect the rich and ensure that their hold on power remains secure. Haiti's wealthy know how tenuous their position is and take whatever steps are required to stay at the top of the pecking order. Whatever other frivolities fill their lives, the luxury of self-deception is not among them.

Down the mountain in Port-au-Prince's slums, the Haitian poor also have no illusions about what the future holds for them. We Americans cherish tales of people who rose from humble circumstances by "lifting themselves up by their bootstraps"—even though America's poor are less likely to rise out of poverty than the lower classes of Canada, Denmark, and France, and even though American class mobility has decreased since the 1970s.[1] Our cultural myth holds that everyone has an opportunity for advancement if they put in enough effort at school and in the workplace. This is hardly the case in Haiti. There, public education is free—but the costs of uniforms, textbooks, and school supplies are beyond the reach of most struggling parents. As a result, only 65 percent of the elementary-school-aged children are enrolled in Haiti's primary schools; of this number, only 35 percent will graduate, while only 20 percent of eligible children will enroll in secondary education.[2] Those who are lucky enough to complete their schooling will find little in the way of opportunity; more than two-thirds of Haiti's labor force do not have formal jobs.[3]

Historically Haiti's rich have flaunted their wealth in the face of poverty, making little pretense of caring about Haiti's poor, openly disparaging them as "savages" and "peasants." If the wealthy thought about the plight of the poor at all, they blamed it on the poor's stupidity and superstition, with such beliefs as "Instead of working hard to earn a living, [the poor] would rather give their money to witch doctors and dance around fires at Vodou ceremonies." According to the rich, any money spent trying to improve the lot of the poor would be money wasted. The destitute have not been seen as suffering countrymen to be uplifted but as a threat that must be contained by any means necessary.

It is easy enough to condemn this system as a moral outrage. It goes against everything we hold dear; there is no pretense of justice or fairness. But before we engage in finger pointing, we might wish to consider how our society deals with its poor. In America most people fancy themselves members of the "middle classes." And along with these beliefs, many hold to their corollary: if you are poor, it is not because of injustice or inequality but because there is Something Wrong With You.

Blue-collar workers and middle-management executives alike often are quick to condemn "welfare mothers" and "illegal immigrants" who leech off hardworking taxpayers. These statements not infrequently rely on the same racist rhetoric that Haiti's light-skinned wealthy use for the poor black population. The resemblance is not coincidental: like those wealthy Haitians, we Americans fear that which might threaten our privilege. And like those Haitians, we use our political clout (and armed guards) to make sure that those threats are contained and kept in their place. If our police are less brutal than the Haitian military, perhaps it is only because our poor are less desperate and hungry.

Thanks to our relative prosperity and easy access to credit, we have been able to provide most of our less fortunate citizens with many of the trappings once associated with wealth. Large televisions, large automobiles, and large homes were once available with no money down. It was easy to pretend you were rich until the credit card bills came due— and even then you could console yourself by thinking of all the millions of others who were living beyond their means. In time, we came to believe this was the order of things; the dream of a better future became a demand for instant gratification. Today we are all paying the price for that long spending binge, as we awaken to a world where working-class mortgage holders and investment bankers alike find that their liabilities are greater than their assets.

As we struggle to right a financial system teetering on the brink of collapse, we may find ourselves redefining what it means to be "middle class." Some may look to socialist models or to postwar and post-Depression ideals. Others may look to Haiti to see a more sinister view of our possible future: a very few members of the upper classes and a great number of poor people. In Haiti, there has been little in the way of a middle class since the 1950s, when the rise of François "Papa Doc" Duvalier led to a mass exodus and "brain drain" that sent most of Haiti's best and brightest to America, Canada, and France. Haiti's poor have no opportunity to buy the trinkets and trappings that would make them feel rich. Those who are rich do not have the luxury of a pacified population. Before we condemn Haiti's society as cruel and inhumane, we may wish to consider what ours would look like if our resources were as limited. Do we have a kinder and more equitable society because we are morally superior, or because we have more disposable income?

Entitlement and You

If the answer to this question is the latter, think about what this means for any feelings of entitlement you may harbor. (First, of course, you must accept that you do harbor feelings of entitlement. We all love to rail against "trust fund kids" and "spoiled brats"; but recognizing our own unrealistic expectations and unjustified self-confidence can be more challenging.) If you are relying on your family's riches, remember that you are one good argument away from being cut off. If you expect your advanced degrees will help you make it through tough times unscathed, consider the fate of those who have been "downsized" or "outsourced" when their knowledge becomes obsolete or available elsewhere at lower prices. If you expect continued growth in your business, contemplate the fates of those who believed that real estate, tech stocks, or tulip bulbs would increase in value forever.

This is not intended to send you into a panic. Panic is a useless emotion: those who panic either freeze up and do nothing or act rashly and foolishly out of desperation. Instead of getting frightened, get prepared. Make sure you have something put aside for hard times. Take pains to make sure that your skill set is current and your knowledge up to date. Do not expect that you can rely on any safety net that you have not woven yourself, and be aware that there is no social contract that guarantees your continued success. Complacency is the harbinger of failure; healthy concern and active planning for all contingencies will help safeguard your status and your money.

If you are looking for work, do not be afraid to take a job that seems beneath you. Haitian Vodouisants know that rice and beans on your plate today will satisfy your hunger better than the promise of a five-course meal tomorrow. Is working at a menial job more shameful than relying on the generosity of your family or the government? You can always find something better—or save your pennies and relocate to an area where more suitable employment can be found.

Don't assume that you have a divinely given right to own the same flashy toys as your neighbors and colleagues. If you can't afford them, chances are good that they can't either. In 2008, the average American household's monthly debt obligations were 130 percent of their discretionary income.[4] Living within your budget may mean foregoing the newest car in your company parking lot or the biggest house on your block—but it will also mean foregoing ruinous interest rates and crippling obligations for things you neither earned nor needed.

Our society screams about "nepotism" when someone uses family or political ties to get ahead (after all, this challenges our cherished Myth of Equality). We would condemn as hypocritical or mercenary someone who too blatantly uses religious affiliations for social or business purposes; to us this betrays the righteous group for the unclean purpose of individual gain and empowerment. Family ties and club circles reek of the "good ol' boys" network; they remind us that others out there may have advantages over us. More discomfortingly, they remind us that we have advantages over many others. While our Myth of Equality allows for and indeed cherishes a starring role for the underdog, it has particular contempt for the spoiled rich kid.

Instead of acting out to rid ourselves of the sinful stigma of inherited wealth and social connections, we might do better to own our advantages and use them without hesitation and without shame. Do not assume that they are some birthright you deserve by virtue of having the right genetics. Rather, understand that those connections are a powerful and useful tool, and that you are very fortunate to have access to them. Don't rely on them as your sole means of support, but don't reject them out of hand in an effort to prove that you're really just "one of the folks." By the same token, don't feel obligated to pick up tabs and buy gifts for people to win their affection. If you wish to absolve yourself of the sin of wealth, there are better penances than buying drinks for the house. Devote your money and time to improving the world rather than purchasing the attention of "friends."

If your sense of entitlement has run headlong into the unyielding wall of reality, this may be a good time to take stock of yourself. You might be feeling very angry at the cold cruel world that has failed to recognize your worth. You may even want to look at some spells to get back at the boss who wronged you or the supervisor who refused to overlook your trivial infractions. There is certainly precedence for this in Vodou: many houngans and mambos will work malevolent magic for a client if the price is right. But it may be more profitable to focus your energies on bettering your current position rather than avenging old slights. There's some truth to the old cliché about living well being the best revenge. You may want to try the "Planning Your Future with General Ogou Badagri" ritual (see chapter 12) to discover where you could have done things differently and make arrangements to avoid these problems in the future. (In general, you will find that Ogou is a marvelous teacher when it comes to overcoming self-delusion. He may be as harsh as a drill sergeant, but he's every bit as effective at shaping you up and teaching you how to earn your success.)

Should you wish to work with the spirit world, you will definitely need to "get over yourself." Author and shaman Raven Kaldera has complained of people who treat the gods like the Big Barbie Who Gives You Stuff. These spoiled sorcerers assume that the deities and demigods have nothing better to do than wait hand and foot on their followers. They react with horror to the idea that the gods may actually demand something in return for their work, or that the gods might show some emotion besides unconditional loving acceptance. If these sorcerers are fortunate, the gods ignore them; the unlucky ones manage to make spirit contact, only to discover that the gods didn't show up to worship them.

Ordering the lwa about is not going to get you very far, neither is making unreasonable requests. A washerwoman might ask for a bit of additional business. If she then made three dollars a day instead of two dollars, she would think herself blessed and give thanks to her patron spirits. She would not complain because they did not give her a laundromat; she would understand that the lwa can only act "as God wills." Many aspiring magicians expect that their spells will solve all of their problems and provide them with lives of unending bliss. They ignore modest but very real changes for the better, always expecting the "great shift." When it doesn't occur, they often throw temper tantrums at the spiritual world, like children convinced that their parents don't love them when there is no pony among the pile of presents beneath the Christmas tree.

Before you ask for that promotion, make sure you have a realistic chance of getting it. You may think that your genius is self-evident, but those responsible for hiring you may not be so sensitive to these things. You will have to prove yourself to them; you may even have to "pay your dues." The lwa may well be able to help you shine at your job, they may even help you to achieve things against overwhelming odds. But don't expect that they will perform miracles on your behalf while you sit back and wait for the perfect job offer. You will find that magic works best when combined with hard work and mundane efforts.

Finally, be aware that there's a difference between feelings of entitlement and healthy self-confidence. Assuming that you deserve preferential treatment is bad; so too is assuming that you deserve to be exploited. Knowing your true worth and expecting others to treat you with proper respect is perfectly appropriate. But understand that you may have to show that worth through hard work and that you may not rise to the top overnight. This doesn't mean that you should tolerate abuse or that you shouldn't seek a better opportunity if your current position is unsatisfactory. But do so with clear eyes and an understanding of what your skills are worth in the current marketplace. Like the U.S. military, the lwa will help you to "Be all you can be." The spirits won't make you a great tycoon when you are qualified to be a great bricklayer, nor will they coddle or give you more than you are capable of earning.

3
Magic and Healing

Bondye do ou, fe pa ou, M a fe pa M. (God says, Do your part and I'll do mine.)

HAITIAN PROVERB

IF YOU'VE BEEN RAISED on a steady diet of Hollywood and fantasy fiction, you may think of magic as something outside of the natural realm. Like Harry Potter disapparating or Aladdin's genie bending reality with a snap of his fingers, you may expect a true spell to have spectacular, life-changing effects. You'll be much more successful—in both the magical and mundane worlds—if you treat magic as another tool that you can use for success. Magic is a supplement to common sense and hard work, not a replacement for them.

Houngans and mambos know this well. Clients with financial difficulties want something simple and direct: more money. It would be easy enough to whip up a money-drawing wanga and send them off. But it will be far more useful, in both the short and long term, to figure out exactly what is causing the client's money woes. The best houngans and mambos look at magic with a holistic eye. They act not only as sorcerers but as counselors, providing useful advice along with their spells and prayers.

If you are reading this book, you presumably feel that you are not as successful as you could be. You may be teetering on the brink of bankruptcy and homelessness; you may feel trapped in an unsuccessful and unfulfilling job; you may be doing well but think you should be doing better. Whatever your situation, you've decided that you need to throw a little magic into the mix. You may be able to improve your condition by doing every spell in this book and hoping that at least one works. But you'll get much better results by determining what is holding you back and concentrating your work on those problems.

To do this, you will first need to follow the counsel of Socrates: Know thyself. This will require sitting down and making an honest inventory of your strengths and weaknesses. What have you accomplished, and what do you hope to accomplish in the future? What were your greatest successes and your greatest failures? What do you hope to gain from practicing Vodou money magic? Write down the answers to these questions in a notebook that only you will see, and be as honest as you possibly can. Don't justify your mistakes, but don't feel obligated to blame yourself for circumstances that truly were beyond your control or to minimize your triumphs over adversity.

Once you have this list in hand, you will have a better idea of what is moving you forward and what is holding you back. You may see positives that you can accentuate, and negatives that can be eliminated. Following are a few difficulties that you might discover. This is by no means a comprehensive list: there is no shortage of reasons why you may be having money difficulties. But it will give you some idea of things you can look for and ways to address those issues.

Compulsive Spending

We joke about "retail therapy"—lifting ourselves out of a blue funk with a trip to the mall. According to a popular bumper sticker, "The one who dies with the most toys wins." Consumer spending accounts for more than two-thirds of America's gross national product (GNP).[1] After the terrorist attacks of September 11, 2001, politicians even spoke of our patriotic duty to lift the economy out of a slump by shopping. As with other indulgences, most can enjoy an occasional frivolous purchase.

But for some, that enjoyable pastime becomes a compulsion that brings more pain than pleasure.

Do you spend a lot of money on things you don't need and didn't even want all that much? Do you find yourself looking at your monthly credit-card statements and wondering, "Why did I buy that anyway?" Do you hope that the lwa can help you with a mountain of debt you incurred on various shopping sprees? If so, you may be dealing with an impulse control disorder that manifests itself in compulsive spending. You're not alone: an estimated 5.8 percent of the U.S. population shops impulsively and is plagued by post-purchase remorse, guilt, and financial woes. For many this condition leads to broken relationships, job losses, and financial ruin.[2]

Compulsive shoppers often describe a "rush" of arousal and a release from the unpleasant feelings that generally build in the hours and days before a shopping expedition. But after buying an item, their guilt and remorse tend to set in quickly. The purchases are often stowed in the back of a closet or in a basement, their price tags never removed. Meanwhile, the desire for another shopping "fix" sets in and the cycle continues.

If you ask the lwa for a windfall to help you with mounting bills, they may answer your petition. But if you are a compulsive buyer, this will only be a short-term gain; before long you will once again find yourself with mounting bills and closets full of unopened items. Extra money will not cure a compulsive shopper any more than extra beer will cure an alcoholic. To make lasting improvements in your financial condition, you will need to address the underlying causes of your problem.

First, you need to understand why you are compelled to spend money. Women who suffer from compulsive shopping disorder generally buy clothes, jewelry, makeup, and gifts for other people—objects of self-adornment that they imagine will enhance their image in the eyes of others. Male compulsive shoppers tend to be "collectors" of things like electronics, CDs, watches, pens, books, and cars. Men tend to engage in compulsive buying when they feel agitated, angry, or elated; women, by contrast, are more often triggered by feelings of depression or boredom. While 80 percent of the persons who seek therapy for compulsive shopping are female, therapists believe that men are just as likely to suffer from the disorder but are less likely to seek treatment.[3]

The "Curb Impulse Spending with Damballah" ritual (chapter 8) can help you get an immediate handle on your problem. You may also benefit from therapy, counseling, and/or medication. A few psychiatric studies have shown that SSRI (selective serotonin reuptake inhibitor) antidepressants, such as fluoxetine and citalopram, can help those suffering from obsessive-compulsive disorders. Most important, you need to understand that no amount of spending will help fill that inner emptiness and bring the happiness that you crave. By adjusting your expectations and seeking satisfaction elsewhere—in your family, in your accomplishments, or in your spiritual life—you may find yourself able to break the cycle of overspending.

Substance Addiction

Many who "Just say no to drugs" have no problem with an occasional drink—or a frequent one. According to a 2002 report by the National Institute on Alcohol Abuse and Alcoholism, 17.6 million Americans age eighteen and older—8.46 percent of the population—are either full-blown alcoholics or abuse alcohol in a fashion "characterized by failure to fulfill major role obligations at work, school, or home; interpersonal social and legal problems; and/or drinking in hazardous situations."[4] You may be convinced that you don't have a drinking problem and may even cite a whole bunch of reasons why you're not an alcoholic: You don't drink alone, you only party on weekends, you never drive drunk, you can quit any time you want. . . . These and many other excuses are part of every substance abuser's litany.

Unfortunately, excuses can become as addictive as your drug of choice. It becomes easy to blame your job failures on that nasty boss (or a long string of nasty bosses) rather than your chronic absenteeism.

Instead of taking responsibility for your behavior, it becomes tempting to play the charming rogue: you're not a failure because you abuse alcohol or other substances, you're just a square peg that doesn't fit into those boring, conventional round holes. Just look at your interest in magical and spiritual things: None of those boring mundane folks at your office can understand that, even if they do show up at their desks on time and avoid snorting cocaine on their lunch hour.

If you have substance abuse issues, you will need to deal with them before your money magic will have any long-lasting effect. Depending on your career, this may be difficult. While the "three martini lunch" is history, many deals are still made over cocktails. Those who work in the entertainment or restaurant industries may be especially likely to encounter temptations on their road to recovery. Although you may have some awkward moments as the only sober person at the office Christmas party, you will soon find the benefits of sobriety far outweigh the occasional discomforts.

Tally up what you spend on your addiction in a given month. You may be unpleasantly surprised to discover just how much of your paycheck is going to feed your habit. Now think of some things you could do with that money instead of supporting your favorite bar or your local dealer. How long would it take you to clear all your outstanding debts? How long until you could put a down payment on a house? How much could you put aside for your children's college education—or your own?

Early on there is often a grim joylessness to recovery; you may feel like you have given up your favorite pastime and have little to show for your sobriety but boredom. But by setting a goal, you will see tangible evidence of how abstinence is working for you. It will seem less like a thankless chore and more like an investment in your future—which of course it is!

You may also be surprised to learn how much more energy and focus you have once you get clean and/or sober. If you have been able to hold your present job while maintaining an active addiction, you may well find yourself on the fast track to promotion once you are clean. You will find that mornings at the office are much more pleasant when you aren't dealing with a raging hangover. You may even discover that you finally have the drive to get out of your dead-end position and seek a better line of work, rather than self-medicating your discontentment. It is far easier to achieve success, magically and otherwise, with a clear head.

You will also find that many of the skills you learned during your days as an active addict will come in handy in the business world. You've got experience in making excuses (otherwise known as "coming up with plausible explanations"). You have learned how to charm your way out of trouble and have mastered the art of working while you're not feeling your best. You may want to cut yourself off from your addict past and reinvent yourself as a clean and sober person. Separating yourself from fellow addicts and favorite watering holes is definitely advisable. But Vodouisants know that no tree grows without roots and that we can never make an entirely clean break with our past. Instead of denying your former addiction, why not make it work for you?

This is a good time to make "A Clean Start with Legba" (chapter 7). It's also a good time to seek out a local Twelve Step group, or, if necessary, hospitalization or an inpatient or outpatient substance abuse treatment center. Addiction is a serious disease; if left untreated it can kill you and cause great suffering to your family, friends, and loved ones. I speak from experience here: I am a recovering alcoholic who took my last drink on October 28, 1995. If you are suffering from this disease, you owe it to yourself and your loved ones to get help and get it now.

Financial Issues with Your Partner

Perhaps you spend frugally, but your spouse keeps running up credit card debt; or, you work two jobs while your live-in partner sits on the couch and plays video games. Indeed, you may have built up a whole narrative around your situation, wherein you play the unappreciated breadwinner who struggles mightily against a cold and uncaring world. And because reality typically meets our expectations, you are likely to remain unappreciated until you take charge of the situation.

If your financial issues can be laid at the feet of your significant other, why are you still together? What are you getting out of the relationship? Don't respond with "She wouldn't be able to survive on her own!" or "He wouldn't know what to do without me!" The question here is not about why you have to meet your partner's needs, it is about what your partner is doing to fulfill yours.

For those who suffer from codependency, it may be difficult even to ask that question, never mind answer it. From an early age they have been taught to disregard their own needs and concentrate on others. They have learned to place the health, welfare, and safety of others before their own: their sense of self-worth is wrapped up not in who they are but in what they can do for others. Codependents gain control in a relationship by giving up control: they put themselves in the role of martyr and force their beloved into the role of burden. This frees the codependent persons from owning their own problems; instead of taking responsibility for their own troubles, they can point to their partner or parent as the reason their life is unsatisfactory and unfulfilling.

If you find it too difficult to ask "What am I getting out of this relationship?" you can ask another question: What would I do if my partner were to change? Codependents often talk at length about how much they wish their spouse would quit drinking, gambling, or engaging in other self-destructive behaviors. But when their partner decides to change, the codependent often responds with subconscious or conscious efforts to sabotage the other's recovery. If the idea of a financially responsible spouse frightens you, you need to think about that. You may be used to playing the role of an alternately indulgent and nagging parent to a problem child, but are either of you comfortable or happy in that drama? Will financial security make your relationship stronger, or will it force you to confront the issues that you have been subsuming in your constant bickering about money?

If you really want to improve your situation, you are likely to encounter some resistance from your partner. The "Soothing Troubled Waters with Agwe" method (chapter 9) may help to ease some of the tension. Counseling may also be in order; both of you will benefit from a mediator who is willing to listen to your concerns and offer helpful suggestions. Twelve Step groups such as Codependents Anonymous may help. If, like many codependents, you were raised in an alcoholic household, you may benefit from attending Adult Children of Alcoholics or Alanon meetings. You can also call on Damballah for peace and healing: he will provide you with guidance and give you the strength to do what must be done.

Ultimately, though, you will have to understand that you will only regain power over your life when you understand that you are powerless over your partner's life. If your partner is willing to change and makes real efforts in that direction, your relationship may have a chance. If your efforts are met with hostility or indifference, you can expect that your financial problems will continue no matter what kind of magic you do. There are many love spells, but there are none that will turn a slacker into a responsible breadwinner or cure a compulsive spender who doesn't want to be helped. Magic, like politics, is the art of the possible. There are no guarantees that your partner will change if you cease to enable his or her misdeeds—but it's a pretty sure bet that if you keep doing what you've always done, you'll keep getting what you've always received.

Family Burdens

Perhaps you have big city dreams but you're stuck in your small town caring for your elderly parents. Or you'd like to return to school, but you're raising a child with no child support. Like George Bailey, Jimmy Stewart's character in *It's a Wonderful Life*, you may feel trapped in a life you never chose and stymied every time you try to escape. So you have decided to turn to Vodou money magic in hopes that you can get out of your rut and make things better for you and the people who rely on your support.

Vodou is certainly a family-centered tradition. Ancestors are honored and children are seen as a great blessing. The idea that one might willfully be "childfree" is inconceivable to many Haitians. But Vodouisants also know that you cannot take care of others unless and until you take care of your own needs. The best way to make a better life for your loved ones is to make a better life for yourself.

Do you want your relationship with your dependents to be based on guilt and resentment, or on love and mutual respect? If you feel you are sacrificing everything for your children or your parents, then you are probably giving them that message in your words and actions. This dynamic may have been ongoing for years, possibly for your entire life. It will be hard to get out of the habit of nailing yourself to the cross; you may encounter resistance from people who are used to being the center of your world. You will have to let them know that you love them and will offer them as much care as you can—but you also have to meet your own needs.

That means you must be able to distinguish between their needs and their desires. You will need to be firm with your boundaries. You will have to stop going without medical care so that your child can have as many toys as everyone else in his class, or neglecting your social life so you can entertain your elderly mother who refuses to go to the senior center and socialize with her peers. This change in priorities is likely to cause tension at first. Spend some time meditating with Danto (see chapter 13) and ask her for advice on how you can show your love without being a doormat.

You can help those who rely on you by encouraging them to be as independent as possible. Teach your children the value of money by giving them a fixed allowance and encouraging them to save for those fashionable sneakers; make that allowance contingent on their completing their chores. This teaches them the value of money and saves you added labor when you get home from your job. If they are of age, let them get a job for their spending money. They will treasure the things that they want enough to work for far more than the things you give them.

Encourage your parents to take advantage of opportunities offered by local senior groups or church organizations. Don't overdo it—you're not helping, for example, by giving your shortsighted and forgetful grandmother the car keys when she insists on driving. But don't let your parent fall into the role of invalid or assume that old age must be a long, slow decline into senility and decay. Reduced cardiovascular function, muscle wasting, and bone loss are no longer considered a natural part of aging but a result of inactivity. Yet only about one-fifth of our current elderly population is physically active at a level that upgrades heart health.[5]

This also applies if you are supporting a child with disabilities or special needs. You may be afraid of letting your son with Down's Syndrome or your autistic daughter out into the world: you know the special agony of hearing your child taunted by cruel and ignorant people. But you must also remember that you may not always be there for them: if you go by actuarial tables, your child is likely to outlive you. By giving them the training and self-confidence to join the workforce or to live with minimal or no assistance, you provide them with survival skills that will ensure they can care for themselves after you are gone. Ask Ogou (chapter 12) to protect them and give them the strength they need to deal with the unkindness of others; also ask him to give you the courage to let go and let your children achieve what they can.

Smart Vodouisants know their limits. Many elderly people fear being institutionalized in long-term care; they may be terrified of strangers, particularly if they are suffering from dementia. This causes them to place increasing demands on their families in an effort to maintain their independence. Their relatives may mean well and do their best to help—but good intentions are no substitute for training in gerontological nursing. As a result, the elderly often suffer needlessly as a result of poor diet, insufficient exercise, lack of stimulation, over or under medication, or self-defeating expectations. If you cannot meet the burden of caring for your relatives, there is no shame in seeking help. Ask Legba (chapter 7) to assist you in finding the services you require and ask Ogou (chapter 12) to grant you the courage to do that which must be done.

If you are having problems getting support for your child, Danto can be a particularly powerful ally. A single mother herself, Danto takes a special interest in children and will do whatever she can to see that their needs are met. Burn a red candle for her and ask for her assistance. You can also use the "Danto's Child Care Agency" spell found in my book *Vodou Love Magic* (Destiny Books, 2009). Of course, you should also call on your local authorities and put them on the case. The lwa can work wonders, but courts can garnish wages and bank accounts.

Spiritual Obligations

In Haiti the lwa will often claim people and demand their service. The person called may be a devout Evangelical Christian, who has never set foot inside a peristyle or attended a Vodou ceremony. This is no matter to the spirits. They will haunt the individual with bad dreams, bad health, and increasing bad luck until such time as the person agrees to provide the lwa with their demands—such as a party, a *maryaj lwa* (mystical marriage to one or more spirits), or an initiation. This may seem distasteful to those of us who prefer that the gods respect our free will. But Vodouisants have long known that the divine is not particularly concerned with getting our permission.

A number of shamanic cultures have described what modern practitioners have come to call "shaman sickness." This sickness is typically a breakdown in mental and physical health combined with bad luck in all other endeavors, and it will continue until such time as the shaman-to-be accepts the calling and begins the necessary training. Resistance will only be met with continued suffering and ultimately may even lead to death. While shaman sickness is rare, it is not unheard of; a number of magicians, including myself, have experienced it.

If your money woes are just one part of a tapestry of troubles, and are combined with persistent visions, voices, and uncanny occurrences, you may be suffering from shaman sickness. Before diagnosing yourself as a shaman-to-be, you should address any possible mundane explanations. Afterward, you should speak with a qualified shaman who is capable of recognizing this condition and providing some steps you can take to pacify the spirits. This is a serious diagnosis and is not to be made lightly—certainly not on the basis of a couple of paragraphs you read in a book.

If you have previous experience with doing magic, have you made any promises to a spirit in exchange for its aid? If you received that aid, did you follow through or did you ignore your obligations? You may think that because your original promise was made casually or out of desperation that you cannot be held to it. ("Sure, if they don't fire me I promise I'll never drink again" or "but I was hungover!") The spirits, alas, think differently. For them a deal is a deal: you promised them you would do something and now they expect you to follow through on it. You may be able to renegotiate, but you will not be able to continue ignoring their demands. Until you have made things right with them, your problems will only get worse.

You also may be dealing with spirits whom you have offended. Contrary to popular belief, the spirit world is not all-loving, all-benevolent, and all-forgiving. To this day many Europeans hesitate to disturb spots that are known to be "elf-homes" or "faerie cairns." Those who scoff at this superstition may learn that although they don't believe in the Good Folk, the Good Folk believe in them. The lwa (and most other spirits) are generally quick to signal their disapproval, but those who aren't listening may find themselves on the receiving end of a Cosmic Smackdown. If you have deliberately or accidentally insulted a god or spiritual entity, you will need to make things right with that entity. Until those spirits are propitiated, they will continue to plague you with bad luck.

If you are suffering from these types of problems, chances are that you know it already. Offended spirits are rarely shy about airing their grievances; they will pop up in dreams and omens to inform you of their disfavor. If you are aware of what you did to get yourself into this pickle, you probably have a pretty good idea of what you need to do to fix things. If not, a reading with a competent and ethical diviner (or a priest of the divinity in question) is in order. But giving a storefront psychic large sums of money to remove your curse won't help; accepting responsibility for your actions and rectifying the problem will.

This may require considerable effort on your part. You may find that you are going to be held to your casual oath from now on, despite your best efforts to evade it. You may have to plant several dozen new trees to make up for the nice old tree you cut down in your back yard. You may even have to start concentrating on your spiritual life and affairs. It won't be easy—but if you have a competent professional on your side, it may be considerably less difficult. In Haiti, houngans and mambos spend a great deal of time helping their clients "get right" with their spirits. Acting as intercessors and mediators, these priests and priestesses help spirit and client alike to achieve a mutually satisfactory resolution to their problem. It helps to have a professional on your side in spiritual and mundane matters alike.

PART TWO

✳

Roots

WE MAY KNOW THAT the wealthiest colony in the Caribbean became the poorest nation in the Western Hemisphere—but do we know how it got that way? And do we know how the Haitian people have responded to two centuries of governmental neglect, foreign oppression, and ever-present grinding poverty?

We may also know that Vodou is based on African folk and religious traditions. But how much do we really know about the system that brought them to the New World? And do we recognize the other streams of practice that fed into Haitian Vodou?

Vodou money magic is more than just isolated chants and spells; it involves deep and long-lasting changes that go beyond the surface. If you don't know where you have been, you will never figure out where you are going. The better you understand Vodou's roots, the more effectively you will use Vodou to your advantage.

4

The Slave Trade

Slaves were awakened at five in the morning by the sound of the commandeur's whistle or by several cracks of his whip or, on the large plantations of over a hundred slaves, by a huge bell. After the recital of perfunctory prayers by the steward, slaves began work in the fields until eight, were allowed to stop for a meager breakfast, and then returned until noon. The midday break lasted until two, when they returned at the crack of the whip to labor in the fields until sundown. On many plantations slaves were forced at the end of the day to gather feed for the draft animals, often having to travel considerable distances from the plantation. Finally, firewood had to be gathered, and dinner, consisting of beans and manioc or a few potatoes, but rarely, if ever, any meat or fish, had to be prepared. During the grinding season on the sugar plantations, slaves then faced what must have seemed like interminable hours of night work at the mills, or of husking and sorting on the coffee plantations.

CAROLYN FICK, *THE MAKING OF HAITI*[1]

WE'RE ALL FAMILIAR WITH the stock images: shackles and chains and human cargo herded into slave ships. Most are thankful that the days of the Middle Passage are gone, and are happy to condemn slavery in Sudan, Somalia, or wherever else this evil may once again rear its ugly head. Certainly the Atlantic slave trade is dead and unmourned. We might remember it as a monument to our cruelty in a dim, distant era or we may wish to forget it altogether.

Alas, the dead don't always rest in peace. Three centuries of brutality and genocide cannot be undone with kind words; the wreckage that the Atlantic slave trade left in its wake will not be repaired solely by our sincere regrets. If we are going to heal, we must first recognize the scope of this disease and understand that we are still sick with its poison. George Santayana's statement that "Those who cannot remember the past are condemned to repeat it" has become a cliché, but that does not make it any less true. If we wish to learn about the power of money, we must understand the lengths to which people will go to acquire it and the atrocities that they will ignore or justify to preserve their creature comforts.

The Slave Trade Begins

In 1500, Portuguese explorer Pedro Álvares Cabral landed in what is today Porto Seguro, Brazil. Soon settlers were flocking to this new land in search of wealth. They brought with them sugarcane (*Saccharum* spp.), an Asian grass that had been introduced to Europe by the Moors in the eighth century. With sugarcane the Portuguese could produce "sweet salt" (crystallized sugar), a substance in high demand among Europe's fashionably wealthy. At first the cane was less profitable than *brasilwood,* the red dyewood that gave the region its name. But as the European market for sugar grew, so did Brazil's sugar plantations. In Europe sugarcane could only be grown in a few warm sections of the Iberian Peninsula; by contrast, much of Brazil was temperate enough for sugarcane cultivation.

But while sugarcane farming was lucrative, it was also labor-intensive. Slash-and-burn clearing was required to remove the thick Brazilian foliage and prepare the ground for cultivation. When the cane was ready for harvest, laborers wielding machetes and cane knives hacked through the tough stems, leaving the roots for next year's crop. Next, the harvested canes were then crushed by heavy rollers until their sweet juice was secreted. This juice was boiled in enormous pots beneath fires fueled by *bagasse* (the fiber remaining from the crushed stalks) until crystallization resulted.

Efforts to run sugarcane plantations with Indian slaves proved unsuccessful as the Indians died *en masse* from disease, maltreatment, and overwork. Workers from Europe faced similar issues; although they had some resistance to the smallpox and influenza that proved so deadly to Brazil's first people, they were vulnerable to malaria, yellow fever, and other diseases common in the hot, humid climate. African slaves, however, proved more resistant to diseases than either Indians or Europeans. And since many slaves came from subsistence farming or herding cultures, they also had experience with agricultural labor. Accordingly, a boom market developed for African slaves—one that would only expand as the exploitation of the New World commenced.

The concept of slavery was not new. More than four thousand years ago the Mesopotamian Code of Ur-Nammu drew distinctions between the free person (*lu*) and slaves (*arad* and *geme*).[2] Slaves built Rome's roads, rowed its galleys, and fought in its coliseums. As late as the twelfth century, English historian William of Malmesbury wrote of Bristol's slave markets, "You could see and sigh over rows of wretches bound together with ropes . . . daily offered for sale."[3] But this new demand for cheap labor was unprecedented. Millions of people—estimates range from 10 million to more than 200 million—were taken from Africa during the seventeenth through nineteenth centuries.

For those unfortunate enough to be captured, the "New World" brought only bondage and hardship. Others—European and African— made fortunes. The slaves acquired in Africa could be exchanged for rum, sugarcane, coffee, and other New World luxuries that commanded high prices in European markets. Money and goods purchased there could be shipped to Africa. There they could be exchanged for still more warm bodies, thereby perpetuating the cycle.

The Slave Kingdoms

As the eighteenth century dawned, the triangular trade between Africa, Europe, and the New World was booming. The Portuguese were still shipping many slaves from their holdings in the Kongo to their Brazilian plantations. Other European powers were seeking to expand their colonial holdings. Dutch slavers brought human cargo to Suriname, while English colonists built plantations in Jamaica and Barbados using African labor. And while the Europeans were building their empires, so were the kings of Dahomey. In 1645 King Houegbadja declared that each Dahomean king would leave his successor more land than he inherited. By 1724 Dahomey conquered the port of Allada and in 1727 gained control of the Ouidah region.[4]

This fulfilled Houegbadja's decree—and positioned his heirs to grow wealthy from the booming slave industry. Their control of Ouidah gave them access to Portuguese merchants who had been trading there for more than a century, and to captives from the Portuguese-controlled Kongo kingdom. Wars between the Fon people of Dahomey and the neighboring Yoruba people (who had their own slave trade) resulted in a steady stream of both Fon and Yoruba slaves. Meanwhile, French merchants who had been purchasing slaves at Allada since the seventeenth century were more demanding than ever as they sought to build their plantations on the new colony of Saint-Domingue.

Slavery's Impact on Africa

When the slaves were brought, the chiefs took a certain number for themselves and sold them to the buyers. People benefited. If you were not a victim, of course, then you benefitted. Sometimes, even the people themselves became victims. Because it was so inhuman that there was no sympathy between them. If you quarreled with your friend

*and you managed to capture him, you could take him to
the market—to sell him.*

*With hindsight, we feel remorse that these things
happened and our great-great grandfathers took part in
the trade. But at that time it was a normal thing. It's just
like what is happening today. It was a market; people were
buying.*

THE PARAMOUNT CHIEF OF SALAGA, HEAD OF A
GHANIAN VILLAGE THAT WAS ONCE A SLAVE MARKET[5]

The first Portuguese slave ships engaged in coastal raids to capture
slaves, but these were inefficient, and once coastal villagers organized to
defend themselves, increasingly dangerous as well. Instead, Portuguese
captains began to rely not on kidnapping but on trade. Since the eighth
century, Arab and African slavers had been shipping captives to the
Middle East, Persia, and the Indian subcontinent; they were as happy
to sell their human wares to Christians as to Muslims. Ships arrived
in African ports carrying European goods (among the most commonly
traded items were cloth, rum, gunpowder, and weapons). These were
traded for slaves who were then shipped to the New World. Once there,
the slaves were exchanged yet again for sugar, molasses, and rum, which
were shipped back to Europe to begin the triangle anew.

Much as the cocaine trade in South America has destabilized governments and funded a generation of drug lords, the Atlantic slave trade
helped keep tyrants and warlords in power. Only states equipped with
rifles and European weapons were able to defend against aggression
from their neighbors—and those weapons generally were available only
to those participating in the slave trade. In the eleventh century the
King of the Empire of Ghana, a traditionalist, employed Muslim scribes
and administrators in his government; the Muslims, for their part, did
not try and convert the King and his people.[6] But because Islamic law
prohibits enslaving a fellow Muslim, Islamic slavers concentrated their
raids on followers of animist and traditional religions. War became

lucrative; a victorious chieftain could grow rich selling the losers to Europeans. This began a tradition of sectarian and ethnic conflict that has persisted in Africa to this day.

Along the Upper Guinea Coast, slave exports during the latter half of the eighteenth century reduced the regional population and halted growth into the first decade of the nineteenth century. Because male slaves fetched higher prices as laborers, the ratio of men to women dropped to less than eighty men per one hundred women. The African population in 1850 has been estimated to be about half of what it would have been had slavery and the slave trade not been a factor in African history.[7]

The slave trade left African societies dependent upon foreign merchants. Few slave profits were reinvested in capital developments; instead, slaves were traded for brandy, fine cloth, bracelets, and other nonessential items. Skilled artisans were put out of work by a flood of cheap imports. In the late nineteenth century Samuel Johnson wrote of Yorubaland (modern-day Nigeria), a region with a long history of ironwork and blacksmithing: "Before the period of intercourse with Europeans, all articles made of iron and steel, from weapons of war to pins and needles, were of home manufacture; but the cheaper and more finished articles of European make, especially cutlery, though less durable are fast displacing homemade wares."[8] This created a culture of leaders enriching themselves and their cronies at the expense of the general population and started a tradition of underdevelopment and exploitation by outside powers that still continues.

Slavery's Impact on Europe and the New World

After the Portuguese introduced plantations to Brazil, other Europeans followed their lead. Soon British, Dutch, Spanish, and French colonists were setting up sugarcane farms wherever the New World's climate would allow. Colonial powers alternately fought wars and bartered for holdings. In 1655 Britain invaded the Spanish colony of St. Iago and set up its own colony of Jamaica, while in 1677 the Netherlands ceded the colony of New Amsterdam (modern-day New York) to England in exchange for the sugar-rich South American colony of Suriname. When the British Parliament raised the duty on molasses and forbade its import from non-British colonies, French Caribbean planters (and the French government) provided enthusiastic support to the rebels who would later become famous as America's founding fathers.

As the numbers of enslaved Africans grew within the colonies, it became necessary to take steps to keep them from becoming a threat. Hence, laws were passed to keep Africans in a state of servitude. It would be an oversimplification to claim that racism was an invention of the slave trade, because for centuries European governments had discriminated against the Rom (Gypsies), Jews, and other outsiders. But the Atlantic slave trade gave this mindset new power. To justify slavery, European intellectuals painted Africans as inferiors whose lives could only improve under the "civilizing" influence of slavery. In 1758, Swedish biologist Carolus Linnaeus, the father of modern taxonomy, distinguished between Europeans (*Homo sapiens europeaus*) and Africans (*Homo sapiens afer*). Europeans were "white, optimistic, and muscular, gentle, active, very smart, inventive"; by contrast Africans were "black, slow, foolish, relaxed, crafty, indolent, negligent."[9] For centuries other scientists and scholars would follow this lead, with innumerable studies "proving" that Europeans were a superior race based on skull shape, eye color, and other irrelevant (and often fudged) points of data.

Under Islamic slavery, a master could have sexual relations with an unmarried female slave but was forbidden from doing so with a married slave (even if married to another slave). Should an Islamic master have children by his female slaves, they were born free; the slave, as an *umm walad* (mother of a child) could not be sold and would be automatically freed upon the death of her master.[10]

But under the plantation system, since Africans were biologically inferior to Europeans (all the best scientific minds of the time said so!), their shortcomings would be passed down to their children. Hence it would be more prudent to treat half-European children as Africans (albeit particularly clever ones) than to accept them as free and equal citizens of the community. In the words of a 1740 slave code from South Carolina: "All Negroes and Indians (free Indians in amity with this government, and Negroes, mulattos, and mustezoes, who are now free, excepted), mulattos, or mustezoes who are now or shall hereafter be in this province, and all their issue and offspring . . . shall be and they are hereby declared to be, and remain hereafter absolute slaves."[11]

Moreover, blacks were seen as savages, and it was presumed that they had no respect for the sanctity of marriage. Hence, there was no reason for a libidinous plantation master to spare one of his attractive slave girls just because she was already betrothed to someone else. The myth of the "hot-blooded Negro" would become a justification for harsh laws and mob violence: in 1937 John Rankin, a Democratic senator from Mississippi, claimed that an anti-lynching law was really "a bill to encourage Negroes to think they can rape white women."[12]

This time period also witnessed the creation of a monster who will trouble the world's consciousness for centuries to come: the "nigger." The "nigger" is subhuman, primitive, and savage, a slave to passion and lust with little capacity for intellectual development. No baptism would break his chains and no profession of faith would save him from his innate inferiority. A baptized Jew was a Christian; a Christian who made the Shahada was a Muslim; but whatever his faith, an African slave was and always would be, a "nigger." He would forever be outside the bounds of civilized society not because of what he believed but because of what he was. He was no longer a human being with some erroneous religious beliefs; he was farm equipment, property that could be bought by anyone with enough capital.

Slavery's Impact on Haiti

Haiti is famous as the first "Black Republic," the country where African slaves succeeded in throwing off their chains. Although that is certainly an achievement to be celebrated, we should contemplate the terrible cost that Haiti paid—and continues to pay—for that revolution. To do that, we must understand the ways in which Haitian society has replayed many of the dramas from the long nightmare.

There were some five hundred thousand slaves on the eve of the French Revolution, with slaves outnumbering free people by about ten to one. Slavery in Saint-Domingue was notorious for its brutality; slaveholders in the other American colonies would often deal with disobedient slaves by threatening to sell them to Saint-Domingue. To maintain order, harsh punishments were used. Pompée Valentin Vastey, secretary to King Henri Christophe (Emperor Henry I of Haiti) and a slave for more than half of his life, described some of these:

> Have they not hung up men with heads downward, drowned them in sacks, crucified them on planks, buried them alive, crushed them in mortars? Have they not forced them to eat shit? And, after having flayed them with the lash, have they not cast them alive to be devoured by worms, or onto anthills, or lashed them to stakes in the swamp to be devoured by mosquitoes? Have they not thrown them into boiling caldrons of cane syrup? Have they not put men and women inside barrels studded with spikes and rolled them down mountainsides into the abyss? Have they not consigned these miserable blacks to man-eating dogs until the latter, sated by human flesh, left the mangled victims to be finished off with bayonet and poniard?[13]

Haitian independence threw much of the New World into a panic. If Saint-Domingue's slaves could rebel, there was no reason to suppose their brethren in Cuba, Jamaica, and the United States would not follow suit. To isolate this, France, Spain, Britain, and the United States joined in an official boycott of Haitian goods. While smuggling of molasses and other supplies continued, Haiti was effectively isolated from the world markets. With legal trade restricted, merchants willing to put in at Haitian ports could dictate their own terms, further exploiting a country that had already been ripped apart by a decade of civil war.

To end this embargo, Haiti was forced to pay France "reparations" for its losses in the Haitian Revolution. In 1825 President Jean-Pierre Boyer offered France 150 million gold francs as indemnity; he further offered to lower customs duties for French products to half those of any other nation. (This sum has been estimated by the present Haitian government to be $21 billion in current dollars.[14]) Even though France later lowered the indemnity payment to 90 million francs, the cycle of forcing Haiti to borrow from French banks to make the payments chained the black nation to perpetual poverty. Haiti did not finish paying her indemnity debt until 1947. In the meantime, money that could have used to build schools and develop the Haitian infrastructure was diverted to France.[15]

From 1915 to 1934, Haiti was occupied by the United States. To build the necessary military roads, the Marines relied on *corvée,* an old and rarely enforced Haitian law that required Haitian men to dedicate three days of each year to public works projects or else pay a tax. Using this as a pretext, occupation forces forced men to work for months at a time as unpaid laborers in conditions reminiscent of southern America's "chain gangs." Those who attempted to escape were shot. By some estimates, as many as fifty-five hundred Haitians died in these forced labor camps.[16]

Two centuries after the Haitian Revolution, poverty has created a new form of slavery in Haiti. Unable to feed their children, desperately poor parents have been forced to sell them as *restaveks*—child slaves who are frequently subjected to physical and sexual abuse. A 1998 United Nations study estimated that as many as three hundred thousand Haitian children—one out of ten children living in Haiti—are forced into a life of menial labor, denied any opportunity for schooling, and beaten or even killed for the slightest misdeeds. While laws exist forbidding the practice, they are rarely enforced.[17]

Slavery and Responsibility

Many have noted that America's slaves and plantation owners are both long dead. Those who swung the whip and those who felt it on their backs have gone on to their eternal reward; so what is there to be gained by opening old wounds? In the words of Libertarian philosopher Robert W. Tracinski, "An apology for slavery on behalf of the nation presumes that whites today, who predominantly oppose racism and never owned slaves, and who bear no personal responsibility for slavery, still bear a collective responsibility—a guilt they bear simply by belonging to the same race as the slave-holders of the Old South. Such an apology promotes the very idea at the root of slavery: racial collectivism."[18]

This appears compelling at first glance. But it neglects two important points:

- Americans have profited, and have continued to profit, from the groundwork laid by the slave trade. The New World would not exist in its present form were it not for slavery. If you are an American citizen—or if you enjoy goods and services provided by American companies or entertainers—you are reaping the harvest sown by generations of enslaved Africans.
- Africans and African Americans continue to suffer from the damage wrought by the slave trade. Twenty-three percent of African American males in their twenties are either in jail or prison, on parole, on probation, or awaiting trial.[19] Although it possesses abundant natural resources and arable land, Africa is the world's poorest continent and, relative to the rest of the world, is getting poorer all the time.

We hold companies responsible for cleanup costs when they cause an environmental disaster—even when that disaster happened long ago. We don't accept "I wasn't working here then, and neither was my staff. Why should we pay to remove leaky oil drums someone else buried twenty years ago?" as a valid excuse. Yet many consider this an appropriate response to the mess left behind after a three-century campaign of genocide that has caused more misery, death, and suffering than any thousand toxic dumps.

There is also a blurring of the distinction between "collective responsibility" and "collective guilt." Collective guilt involves blame and punishment. Statements such as "Homosexuals spread AIDS" aren't talking points for a discussion about how to rectify a problem. Rather, they are a convenient stick with which to beat a hated group. (Few gay-bashers spend their spare time distributing condoms and clean needles, actions that would be far more likely to limit the spread of AIDS than random assaults on strangers.) Collective guilt is not something a group accepts, but rather is something forced upon them. Collective responsibility, on the other hand, involves recognizing the privileges that you have. It means realizing that your society was built on the suffering and oppression of others—and doing something to pay back that debt.

Being conscious of previous atrocities also helps us to be aware of current ones. Although the outright buying and selling of human beings has become less common than it once was, it has not died out. Neither has child labor, indentured servitude, prison labor, or other forms of quasi-slavery. A 2008 raid on Agriprocessors, an Iowa meat-processing plant, found children as young as thirteen working long hours under hazardous conditions. One sixteen-year-old Guatemalan there described working seventeen-hour shifts, six days a week, and said, "I was very sad and I felt like I was a slave."[20] Many of the items that we have come to associate with "the good life" are made by people working in sweatshop conditions here and elsewhere. Corporations have taken advantage of lax labor laws in other countries to set up factories where they need not concern themselves with issues such as employee safety or prevailing wages. In Colombia, Coca-Cola plant managers have relied on right-wing "death squads" to intimidate, torture, and murder union representatives.[21] In 2005, the International Labor Rights Fund filed suit in Federal District Court in Los Angeles against Wal-Mart, asserting that workers from Bangladesh, China, Indonesia, Nicaragua, and Swaziland were working under conditions that violated the company's code of conduct.[22]

Much as the development of the New World would not have been possible without the rise of the African slave trade, our current standard of living would not be sustainable without the exploitation and abuse of workers around the world. The mass-produced gewgaws that we take for granted are being put together by disempowered laborers in China, Indonesia, Burma, and similarly impoverished places. Where once an industry grew up around trafficking slave labor to plantations, today "globalization" brings the plantations to countries where people are abundant and labor protections rare. While we may make a few piteous noises about "sweatshops," we continue to buy items made under horrendous conditions. Saint-Domingue's colonists were sustained by Europe's ever-increasing sugar and indigo demands. To what extent do we support dictatorships around the world by our greed for the toys that keep us pacified? Before we condemn the excesses of our forefathers, we may do well to examine our own culpability.

5
Christianity

To practice Vodou, you must be Catholic.

HAITIAN PEASANT TO ALFRED MÉTRAUX[1]

MANY SPIRITUAL SEEKERS FROM our culture have a knee-jerk reaction against anything that smacks of Christ. They shy away from crucifixes and bibles like vampires repelled by holy objects. "Christo-fascists" have become a favorite bogeyman among alternative cultures. Conspiracy theorists mutter darkly of the Burning Times every time an evangelical Christian wins an election. Once Satan was blamed for war, famine, and Luther's constipation; today Jesus is held accountable for everything from genocide to sexual repression to bad haircuts among his ministers.

These anti-Christians focus on the many atrocities and abuses committed in Christ's name, but ignore two thousand years of philosophical discourse and mystical techniques. They also ignore ties to the literal "faith of their fathers." This weakens their ties to the ancestors (see chapter 15) and may even cause open hostility with departed kinsmen who resent their descendant's conversion to what they perceive as heathenism and devil worship. Perhaps most important of all, this blinds them to the way Christianity influences their own worldview—starting, perhaps, with their belief in an evil entity whose followers are either deluded or actively malevolent.

No tree grows without roots: we should not be surprised to discover that we have internalized many of the preconceptions and prejudices of Christianity. Even the alternative religious and spiritual traditions that have taken hold in our culture have incorporated many Christian ideas. For example, we speak of "good" and "bad" karma as if we were discussing virtues and sins. But in orthodox Hinduism, all karma—the result of cause and effect—is something to be avoided. This is not necessarily a bad thing, mind you: Christianity may have given us the Crusades and the Inquisition, but it also gave us St. Paul's Cathedral and Michelangelo's David.

While Christian concepts are often a stumbling block to understanding foreign traditions, they can serve as a nexus point between our world and the world of Haitian Vodou. Christian imagery is widely used in Vodou and many Christian legends have become part of the Vodou canon. Peristyles and altars are decorated with statues and images of saints, and holy days on the Catholic calendar are syncretized with lwa *fets* (festivals). Understanding what these symbols mean to Vodou culture—and to your own—will provide a much better grasp of how and why Vodou works.

Vodou, Catholicism, and Saint-Domingue

Although France's Le Code Noir (The Black Code) of 1687 ordered that "All slaves . . . shall be baptized and instructed in the Roman, Catholic, and Apostolic Faith," few were given anything more than a cursory sprinkling with holy water, if that. The antireligious and anti-clerical sentiments that marked much of the French Enlightenment were particularly strong in Saint-Domingue. The colony earned the nickname "Babylon of the New World" for its deplorable moral state.[2] The French had little interest in offering salvation to the slaves they saw as pack animals. They feared Vodou not because it was anti-Christian but because it was a threat to their social order; they had little use for Catholic doctrine or morality in their own lives and even less interest in extending its benefits to the slaves.

This is not to say that the slaves had no knowledge of Christianity. Christian missionaries and merchants had brought the gospel to western and central Africa centuries before the great slave trade began. The Ethiopian kingdom of Axum had converted to Christianity in the fourth century CE while St. Augustine was born and spent much of his life in present-day Algeria. One of the most powerful kings in western and central Africa, King Nzinga of Kongo, converted to Christianity in 1491. Many Kongolese nobles and merchants followed his lead, thereby spreading Christianity across a wide and complex trade network.

Many of the slaves in Saint-Domingue had been Christian before their capture; others were at least familiar with the imagery and basic prayers of the religion. The first Portuguese missionaries to Kongo had translated Christian texts into KiKongo using words such as "spirit," "god," and "holy" rendered directly from existing concepts in Kongo cosmology.[3] By the eighteenth century there was a long tradition of syncretism and symbiosis between African and Christian beliefs in Africa.

If the colonists had no concern for saving their slaves, neither did they feel it necessary to hide their religion. House slaves regularly accompanied their owners to church services; many masters saw to it that their children produced by black concubines were educated and baptized. Catholicism and its trappings came to be associated with sophistication, power, and wealth. Obviously the White God was powerful; one need only consider the incredible good fortune He showered on those who worshipped him. In 1722 French priest Jean-Baptiste Labat complained that:

> The Negroes . . . intermix Dagon's ark and secretly keep all the superstitions of their ancient idolatrous cult with the ceremonies of the Christian religion. In regard to the holy water, the little bit of water that is consecrated during the Sunday Mass, it is rare that one finds one drop of it when the ceremony has ended; they [believe] it will guarantee their welfare against all the witchcraft that might befall them.[4]

The growing class of *affranchis*—free people of color—sought to distance themselves from the African slaves. One way in which they did this was by espousing Catholicism, even though colonial law forced them to sit apart from the whites in church. Another was by joining Masonic lodges (see chapter 6). Both of these strategies for social advancement would play important roles in the war for Haitian independence.

Vodou, Catholicism, and the Haitian Republic

Toussaint Breda L'Ouverture, Haitian revolutionary and ruler of Saint-Domingue from 1797 to 1802, was a devout Roman Catholic who admired French culture and was a devoted follower of Napoleon. Raised and educated by a comparatively benevolent master, L'Ouverture hoped to "civilize" his fellow Africans. After he was betrayed by the French in 1802 and sent to his death in a Swiss prison, Jean-Jacques Dessalines came to power.

Dessalines's service to the lwa, particularly Ogou (see chapter 12), was well known; so was his contempt and hatred for French culture. During the bloody Saint-Domingue revolution, most of the French priests and missionaries were slaughtered alongside their fellow colonists. Those who escaped were understandably reluctant to return after the establishment of Haiti. The Vatican also refused to recognize the Republic or to send clergy to the island. So far as they were concerned, Haiti had reverted to savagery.

Yet this contemptuous rejection did not dampen Haitian enthusiasm. The affranchis were now part of the mulatto propertied class; they retained their devotion to Mass and hoped to see their children educated in Catholic schools. The freed slaves, who occupied a social place somewhere between serfs and landless peasants, were equally interested in Catholicism. They saw the saints, angels, and various virgins as *mistés* (mysteries) like the lwa. Not only were the saints and their images used as representations of African spirits but they were honored in their own right.

Jean-Pierre Boyer, president of Haiti from 1820 to 1843, declared Catholicism the state religion of Haiti. When this did not cause the Vatican to change its position, many adventurers came to Haiti to take up their own version of holy orders. Defrocked priests (and laymen armed with a few books and a basic knowledge of Latin) found a thriving business selling blessings, charms, exorcisms, and other religious services to the people. Even today Haitians who memorize the *priye gineh* (African prayer, or prayer of ancestral Africa, honoring ancestors, the saints, and all of the lwa) and some Catholic rituals can earn money by acting as *prets savanne* (bush priests) and fulfilling priestly roles such as reciting prayers and officiating at a *maryaj lwa* (marriage to the lwa).

In 1860, after more than fifty years of negotiations, a concordat was finally reached between the Vatican and the Haitian government; Port-au-Prince was established as the ecclesiastical center and officially trained priests and missionaries began returning to Haiti. Their presence was welcomed by mulattos hoping to reestablish European standards of culture and civilization on the island. The poor blacks barely noticed. They continued to serve the lwa and the saints by attending Masses; it mattered little to them if the priest railed against "folly and superstition" in a language they did not understand.

For its part, the Church generally supported the mulatto establishment and Haitian wealthy. Private Catholic schools educated a whole generation of upper-class Haitians, caring little for the needs of rural peasants. Any attention paid to the countryside was generally in the form of "antisuperstition campaigns" that sought to eradicate Vodou by arresting prominent houngans and mambos and burning temples, drums, and other signs of "idolatry." But this did not cause Vodouisants to turn away from the Church any more than it caused them to abandon their ancestral practices. Vodouisants have long juggled obligations between various lwa; they have never had any expectation that the spirit world was a morally consistent place.

Christianity, Vodou, and the Duvaliers

Today François "Papa Doc" Duvalier (1907–1971) is best remembered for his ties to Vodou. Yet he was also happy to appropriate Catholic imagery to cement his hold on power, as can be seen in the "Catechism of the Revolution" distributed in Haitian schools during his reign:

> Our Doc, who art in the National Palace for Life, hallowed be Thy name by present and future generations. Thy will be done in Port-au-Prince and in the countryside. Give us this day our new Haiti, and never forgive the trespasses of those traitors who spit on our country each day. Lead them into temptation, and poisoned by their own venom, deliver them from no evil.[5]

Papa Doc understood the importance of Catholicism among the mulatto ruling classes who despised him. He played on the old divisions, presenting Catholicism as a foreign religion ruled by Rome and implying that Catholic mulattos were themselves foreign and less Haitian than *les Duvalieristes*. Yet he was also a wily politician who was willing to work with his enemies. On August 15, 1966, Duvalier's clandestine efforts paid off. In exchange for his guarantee that Roman Catholicism would remain Haiti's official state religion, another papal concordat appointed several pro-Duvalier Haitian bishops and guaranteed that future offices would give preference to "indigenous clergy."[6] But although Papa Doc likely saw this as yet another triumph, it would have unintended consequences after his death in April 1971.

At first Jean-Claude Duvalier seemed a welcome change from his father. The nineteen-year-old "Baby Doc" freed a few political prisoners, restored some press freedoms, and allowed the formation of opposition political parties. But when liberty led to increasing criticism of his regime and its flagrant looting of the Haitian treasury, he took a page from his father's book. Calling on the *Volontaires de la Sécurité Nationale* (VSN, or Volunteers of National Security), better known as the "Tonton Makouts," or Tonton Macoutes,* he launched a campaign of intimidation, repression, and terror.

In the past Haiti's Catholic Church would have greeted this turn of events with silence, if not approval. But the new Haitian clergy—ordained under Papa Doc's concordat—were not so cooperative. Brought up in the country, they spoke Kreyol, the language of Haiti's poor. But whereas the French clergy had concentrated their efforts on the French-speaking elite, Papa Doc's priests focused instead on the black peasants and marginalized city-dwellers. They were encouraged in their efforts by the Second Vatican Council (Vatican II) and by "liberation theology," a movement that encouraged pastors to speak out on social justice issues.

When Pope John Paul II visited Haiti in March 1983, he added further fuel to the fire. At an outdoor Mass the Pope bluntly condemned the unequal distribution of wealth in Haiti, reminded Haiti's elite of their "serious and urgent responsibility with respect to their brothers and sisters," and publicly endorsed the slogan of Haiti's yearlong Eucharistic Congress, "Something must change here." Later, at an address to the Latin American Bishops' Conference in Port-au-Prince, the Pope told the sixty-two assembled delegates, "The poorest must have a preference in your hearts."[7]

This message was taken to heart by *Ti Liglez* (the "little church"), a grassroots movement of Haitian catechists, peasants, and workers. They used Haiti's Catholic radio station, Radio Soleil (Sun Radio), to publicize human rights abuses, vote fraud, and corruption. Duvalier tried repeatedly to silence the radio station by jamming the signal, beating reporters and directors, and engaging in other forms of legal and extralegal harassment. In December 1985 a Haitian government official told

---

*Tonton Macoute translates literally to "Uncle Gunnysack," of Haitian Creole mythology. Uncle Gunnysack was a bogeyman who kidnapped children from the streets after dark and stowed them in a gunnysack, never to be seen again. Likewise, anyone who spoke out against Baby Doc Duvalier would also disappear in the night and never be seen again.

Ti Liglez, "In this battle you will lose because we have weapons and the church has none." But by February 1986, Baby Doc was in exile. His henchmen were hiding from the dechoukage (uprootings) that greeted his fall while the supporters of Radio Soleil cheered in the streets. Among them was a popular Salesian priest who had become famous throughout Haiti for his sermons on Radio Soleil.

Father Aristide Comes to Power

I was walking through La Saline and it was raining. In the rain, in the flood of mud, the cart haulers covered with muddy sweat continued to pull their heavy loads without respite, as usual, doing the work of black slaves. Cart haulers, tragic, Sisyphean figures, condemned to carry eternally the creaking load of the pain of oppression. Can we continue to find this situation of violence that is imposed on the poor, normal?

FATHER JEAN-BERTRAND ARISTIDE[8]

In 1985 Father Jean-Bertrand Aristide led a startling, defiant Mass that called for change in the country, and bluntly criticized the Duvalier regime. Aristide's brash sermon attracted the attention of the foreign press, and was credited by many with sparking the unrest that ultimately led to Baby Doc's departure. In April 1986 Aristide led a march to the notorious Dimanche Prison, where an estimated thirty thousand Haitians were killed during the Duvalier years. The Haitian military opened fire on the praying crowd, but Aristide continued broadcasting on Radio Soleil. This atrocity helped further weaken the ruling military junta's hold on power, and established Aristide's reputation as a fearless critic of the regime.

Critics within the Church were becoming increasingly uncomfortable with the Marxist slant of many liberation theologians. Although the Salesian order was known for its involvement in politics, many Salesians were uncomfortable with Aristide statements such as: "The solution is revolution, first in the spirit of the Gospel; Jesus could not accept people going hungry. It is a conflict between classes, rich and poor." And "We will advance toward the left, where our real Faith, our unshakable belief, can build a socialist Haiti."[9]

But Aristide's critics within the Church were less immediately dangerous than his enemies in the Haitian government. On September 11, 1988, armed thugs descended on St. John Bosco, Aristide's church, during a Mass. In the ensuing riot (which was encouraged by watching police and army members), the church was burned to the ground; thirteen worshippers were killed and seventy wounded. The military might have hoped that the St. John Bosco massacre would intimidate Aristide and his supporters. Instead it outraged them, while Aristide's survival led many of his supporters to credit him with supernatural powers. The attack on a church stripped the established order of any claim to authority. Six days after the massacre a group of young noncommissioned officers ousted ruling General Henri Namphy.

As Aristide gained political power he attracted increasing attention from the Church. In December 1988 he was expelled from the Salesians for "glorification of class struggle, in direct opposition to the teachings of the Church," as well as "using religion to incite hatred and violence."[10] But Aristide remained wildly popular with his supporters, a group he affectionately called "Lavalas" (the flood). In December 1990 the flood swept Haiti's elections, as Aristide handily defeated Marc Bazin (a former World Bank official and the U.S. Administration's favored candidate) for the Haitian presidency. Yet by September 1991, just seven months after taking office, Aristide was in exile, and yet another military leader, General Raoul Cédras, was in charge of Haiti.

Aristide's clerical background worked to his advantage in exile. Diplomats and jaded politicians saw him as a man of God, perhaps even a saint. It also helped that the Haitian Armed Forces and the government-trained paramilitary organization Front Révolutionnaire

Armé pour le Progrès d'Haiti (FRAPH), or Revolutionary Front for Haitian Progress, were engaging in extrajudicial killings, rape and torture of women, and drug dealing. Aristide's tireless efforts and extraordinary personal charisma helped to galvanize ever-increasing U.S. and international pressure against the regime.

In Haiti Aristide remained influential despite the best efforts of FRAPH thugs to intimidate his supporters. In September 1993 gunmen pulled Antoine Izmery, an associate of Father Aristide, out of a memorial Mass commemorating the 1988 massacre and shot him dead in the street. The message, one supporter said, was that "You cannot hide behind a priest's vestments and not even a church offers a safe refuge."[11] But by October 1994 Cédras was on his way to Panama and President Clinton was declaring Father Aristide's return home a victory for freedom and "the beginning of a new era of hope for the people of Haiti."

Aristide Returns to Power

Aristide's relationship with Church officials had been stormy since his days in the Salesians. In August 1994 Haiti's eleven bishops issued a statement saying any military intervention by the United States to restore Father Aristide was "scandalous and immoral" and "makes us tremble with indignation." (For his part, Aristide called the Archbishop of Port-au-Prince "a zealous servant of Macoutism" and stated that any time a bishop "supports generals who murder liberty, he commits a crime.")[12] Not long after his first term as president ended, Aristide asked to be released from his priestly vows, and on January 20, 1996, he married lawyer Mildred Trouillot, the American-born daughter of Haitian immigrants.

But by so doing, Aristide alienated many of his supporters. In resigning from the priesthood, he lost much of the air of sanctity and moral uprightness that had served him so well throughout his career. Said Olrich Charles, a Port-au-Prince sports instructor: "Aristide was already married to the Haitian people. This is like a divorce, only three times: first from his supporters, then from his class, and finally from the church."[13] Father Aristide was a holy man speaking truth against power; but President Aristide looked uncomfortably like yet another Haitian politician seeking to enrich himself and his followers. Soon many of Aristide's followers were noting the authoritarian tendencies his critics in the Church had noted, and they either drifted away from Aristide or became bitter enemies.

It soon became apparent that Aristide's handpicked successor, René Préval, was not going to act as a mere figurehead. Neither were the nascent Haitian opposition parties going to rubberstamp his demands in parliament. But Aristide still remained wildly popular among the poorest of Haiti's poor. Taking a page from Duvalier, he encouraged his *chiméres* (monsters), an independent pro-Aristide militia much like the Tonton Makouts, to attack opposition leaders and lead a "Lavalas Revolution." In 2000 Aristide regained the presidency with 91 percent of the vote in an election marked by widespread accusations of fraud and voter intimidation. Ensuing cuts in foreign aid increased the country's economic woes and led to further unrest. In 2004 Aristide was once again forced out in what he (and many of his supporters) called a "kidnapping" by U.S. forces. He was removed to Jamaica and later settled in South Africa. In 2006 René Préval was returned to the Haitian presidency in a close election.

Evangelical Christianity: The Blood of Jesus Washes Over Haiti

Poverty is not the reason for rapid church growth in Haiti. One of the more important factors is voodoo. This mixture of Christian and pagan beliefs produces a fear of the spirit world. Christ's message is one of freedom from the powers of darkness.

The Haitian church is also a very alive and aggressive

church. There is a big emphasis on effective prayer. Lively congregational singing and special music are important parts of the services. A large percentage of church members are very active witnesses for the Lord. Local churches feel a heavy responsibility for planting sister churches in nearby villages.

HOWARD CULBERTSON, MISSIONARY TO HAITI, 1987[14]

In 1817 Alexandre Pétion asked the Methodists to establish a primary school in Port-au-Prince. By the mid-nineteenth century, there were a number of Protestant missions in Haiti. Staffed largely by African American missionaries, they could be found throughout the Haitian countryside. During the 1915 to 1934 occupation, Haiti came under the direct control of the United States. America had long been a majority Protestant culture, with a long history of anti-Catholic sentiment. It was also a country in the grip of the revival movement, with preachers like Billy Sunday and Aimee Semple McPherson pulling in bumper crowds throughout the nation. Still, their efforts bore little fruit. In 1930, during the U.S. occupation's final years and after a decade of missionary efforts, only 1.5 percent of Haiti's population identified as Protestant.[15]

The year 1950 marked a turning point for the Haitian Evangelical movement. That year Paul and Mary Orjala, young Nazarene missionaries, first arrived in Haiti. The Orjalas would remain there until 1964, establishing and conducting a Bible Training School (*Séminaire Theologique Nazaréen d' Haiti* in Port-au-Prince) that would prepare a generation of native-born Haitian evangelists. Today 70 percent of the Nazarene church membership of the Caribbean region is in the country of Haiti. There are more than one hundred thousand Nazarenes living in Haiti—more than that of any other country in the world with the exception of the United States.[16]

That same year Radio 4VEH, *La Voix Evangelique d' Haiti* (the Evangelistic Voice of Haiti), began broadcasting in Vaudreuil in northern

Haiti. Under the Reverend G. T. Bustin, the East and West Indies Bible Mission (now the Evangelical Bible Ministries) offered broadcasts in French, Spanish, and Kreyol. Where the Catholic clergy spoke French, these ministers offered messages in the language of the local population. They began to attract a growing following among Haiti's poorest. Other radio ministries would follow; today Evangelical groups control many of Haiti's radio stations.

After Papa Doc Duvalier came to power in 1957, he sought a counterbalance against the power of the ever-troublesome Catholic Church. Toward that end, he welcomed Protestant missionaries. Because their visas could be revoked at a moment's notice, foreign pastors generally sought to avoid political entanglements. Under the Duvalier regime, missionaries had a great deal of freedom to build schools and engage in aid projects; so numerous were these groups that by the 1970s any white man traveling in the countryside was likely to be called "pastor" by the local populace. Alarmed by the growth of Protestantism among the poor, many of Haiti's Catholic leaders began distancing themselves from the ruling party while others became part of a growing Catholic populist movement.[17]

Unlike earlier crusades, this one appears to have taken root in country. Today we see an ever-increasing number of Evangelical Protestants within the Haitian and Haitian-American community. Because the mythology of Evangelical Christianity is more dualistic than Haitian folk culture, they can only explain uncanny healings or possessions in terms of "devil worship" and "Satanism." As a result, they are often openly hostile to Vodou. Many see it as bondage to the forces of darkness and a major cause of Haitian violence, injustice, and poverty. By bringing the Good News to their fellows, they hope not only to save souls but to save their country.

There has been self-righteous clucking in the usual quarters about Evangelicals perpetuating acts of "cultural genocide" against Vodou and its practitioners. The relationship between Evangelicals and Vodouisants is certainly tenser than the relationship between Vodouisants and the

Catholic Church. A member of my société comes from an Evangelical family: were they to discover that she serves the lwa, she would be disowned. But we should not neglect the benefits that missionary money has brought to Haiti. Their aid organizations are often better funded, more transparently managed, and more efficient than their secular counterparts—when there *are* any secular counterparts.

A growing number of Haitian Vodouisants have decided that the protection of Jesus is less onerous and costly than the protection of the lwa and family spirits. While *houngan et mambo pas travay pou un granmesi* ("houngans and mambos don't work for a big thank you," that is, they charge for their services), many Evangelical Christian missions offer free health care, education, and other opportunities to those willing to profess the faith. For those converts, Evangelical Christianity offers more powerful and effective magic than Vodou. Vodou has survived many other challenges to its existence, it will be interesting to see how it responds to market pressure from a hostile competitor that seeks to convert, not just pacify, its target clientele.

So What's All This Got to Do with Me?

Some readers will find these slices of Haitian history fascinating; others may wonder just what it has to do with money magic. If you are just memorizing dates, names, and places like you're preparing for a pop quiz, the answer is "nothing at all." But if you are willing to apply this same level of dispassionate scrutiny to your own relationship with Christianity, it may prove to be most enlightening indeed.

Haitian Vodouisants face constant condemnation from Catholic clergy and Evangelical missionaries alike. Yet they practice the "smile and nod" school of diplomacy, rather than return the church's scorn. They agree happily with the priest or the preacher, then serve their lwa when he is gone.

They offer us a good lesson. Perhaps you should take stock of what you gain from publicly proclaiming your membership in an alternative religion or counterculture movement. How much is your aggressive "self-expression" (religious and otherwise) worth to you in lost opportunities? And how much does it help your chosen cause? Are you drawing opposition from people who might otherwise ignore you or even be sympathetic to your ideas?

I would not recommend that anyone proclaim themselves "saved" simply for personal gain. (On the other hand, I'd be lying if I said nobody ever "got religion" for business purposes or that such conversions were never successful.) But it may be worthwhile to ask what is gained by open hostility toward the dominant faith. While our culture may allow public temper tantrums, it rarely rewards them.

Mahatma Gandhi, the Reverend Martin Luther King, the Dalai Lama, Archbishop Desmond Tutu, and other religious leaders have become Holy People of Color to a rapt and well-heeled audience. Their images become icons of saintly dedication and goodness in the face of oppression. By placing them on our T-shirts or in our advertisements, we proclaim our dedication to their cause: our sympathy allows us to bask in the warm glow of moral correctness. At best, this keeps us from hearing the very real and very important messages these leaders have to offer. It defangs their fervor and deflects the challenges they present. At worst, it blinds us to their weaknesses and leads us to overlook or minimize their failings.

In October 1978, French philosopher Michel Foucault said about Iran's revolutionary leader Ayatollah Khomeni: "The situation in Iran seems to depend on a great joust under traditional emblems, those of the king and the saint, the armed sovereign and the destitute exile, the despot faced with the man who stands up bare-handed and is acclaimed by a people."[18]

We may wish to greet claims of sanctity with suspicion. True holiness will survive skepticism. A little bit of research will reveal many spiritual frauds. Aristide's reputation as a firebrand and an autocrat was well established in Haiti before his rise to power. Yet these reports were ignored or dismissed by people who wanted desperately to be in the presence of a living saint and who hoped that Haiti would finally be saved by a miracle. Haitian Vodouisants may expect and regularly experience miracles—but they've long known that you cannot rely on them.

If we want to do money magic, we should examine how the dominant cultural religion has influenced our own attitudes toward money. In European and American culture Christianity's relationship with wealth is generally ambivalent at best. We honor a humble carpenter who said, "It is easier for a camel to go through the eye of a needle than for a rich man to enter the kingdom of God"(Mark 10:25). We are taught that "the love of money is the root of all evil" (1 Timothy 6:10). Prosperity becomes a sign that we are too interested in things of this world—or, in modern parlance, that we have "sold out." Dealing with these internalized issues may help you to overcome self-sabotaging behaviors and claim your success.

Perhaps the most important lesson to take away is this: there is power in Christianity. There is power in its imagery, there is power in its pantheon, there is power in its prayers. While we may decry the excesses and atrocities committed in its name, we cannot deny its long and largely successful history. Nor can we deny the slightly shorter but no less illustrious history of yet another current that has influenced modern Vodou: Freemasonry.

6

Freemasonry

FREEMASONS, n.: An order with secret rites, grotesque
ceremonies, and fantastic costumes, which, originating
in the reign of Charles II among working artisans of
London, has been joined successively by the dead of past
centuries in unbroken retrogression until now it embraces
all the generations of man on the hither side of Adam and
is drumming up distinguished recruits among the pre-
Creational inhabitants of Chaos and Formless Void. The
order was founded at different times by Charlemagne,
Julius Caesar, Cyrus, Solomon, Zoroaster, Confucius,
Thothmes, and Buddha. Its emblems and symbols have
been found in the Catacombs of Paris and Rome, on the
stones of the Parthenon and the Chinese Great Wall,
among the temples of Karnak and Palmyra, and in the
Egyptian Pyramids—always by a Freemason.

AMBROSE BIERCE, *THE DEVIL'S DICTIONARY*[1]

TODAY MOST SEE THE Masons as a bunch of middle-aged men who get together to wear funny hats and declare their brotherhood over several rounds of drinks. Those who remember *The Honeymooners* will recall the International Order of Friendly Sons of the Raccoons; fans of *The Simpsons* will remember the hilarious episode where Homer joins the Stonecutters. Sure, a few conspiracy nuts may tie their local Shriners to the Elders of Zion, Bilderbergers, and Trilateral Commission—but for the most part Freemasonry is an accepted and harmless, if somewhat laughable, part of society.

This was not always the case. From 1827 to 1840 an "Anti-Masonic Party" fielded candidates in many American elections. Among its most prominent members was former president John Quincy Adams. (While the Anti-Masonic Party's crusade against Masonry may have failed, the party created a tradition that survives to this day—the presidential nominating convention.) Many fascist regimes have considered the Freemasons a potent political threat: between eighty thousand and two hundred thousand Masons perished in concentration camps during Germany's Nazi era.[2] Today the links between anti-Semitism and anti-Masonry persist: Saddam Hussein had declared membership in a Masonic lodge "or other Zionist organization" punishable by death, while the organizing articles of Hamas state that Freemasons are "lackeys who are infiltrated through Zionist organizations" and that Freemasonry (like the Rotary and Lions Clubs) is a "sabotage group."[3]

Although evidence linking the Freemasons to the Elders of Zion or alien overlords from *Zeta Reticulati* is shaky at best, Masons have played a prominent role in several revolutions. Freemasons threw the Boston Tea Party—Ethan Allen, John Hancock, and George Washington were all Freemasons. (Of course, so was Benedict Arnold.) After the French Revolution, at least 320 of the 1,336 delegates chosen to the Estates-General are believed to have been Freemasons.[4] And Freemasonry was equally popular in the French colonies, particularly Saint-Domingue.

Freemasonry and Haitian History

As with most things in the colony, Saint-Domingue's Masonic lodges were organized around color lines. From 1784 to 1792 the *Cercle des Philadelphes,* a Masonic society devoted to developing the sciences and arts in the wealthy but culturally lacking colony, claimed many of Saint-Domingue's most prominent white residents as members, along with a few honorary foreign members, most notably Benjamin Franklin (who was also Grand Master of lodges in Paris and Pennsylvania). Those who lacked the social standing to join the Cercle could content themselves with less prestigious lodges. By some accounts, as many as one out of three French colonists in Saint-Domingue were active Freemasons.

Meanwhile, many wealthy affranchis (free blacks) became Masons during sojourns in France, where the fraternities were more racially integrated, and then returned to the colony to found their own organizations. Vincent Ogé (1755–91), a wealthy mulatto and Freemason, traveled to Paris to plead for the rights of *gens du couleur* in Saint-Domingue. When his pleas went unheard, he armed two hundred of his fellow Masons in a 1790–91 effort to overthrow Saint-Domingue's colonial government. Ogé's rebellion, alas, was quickly suppressed and he was sentenced to a particularly brutal death: his arms, legs, hips, and spine were broken with hammers and he was then tied to a wheel and left to die in the sun as a warning to any other affranchis who might wish to rise above their station.

To quell the unrest that arose after Ogé's execution, the French government sent a twenty-nine-year-old barrister named Léger Félicité Sonthonax. His official goals were to enforce the new French law of April 4, 1792, which granted full rights to free men of color. In the face of the ever-growing slave uprising, Ogé's wealthy and educated compatriots appeared less like a malevolent threat and more like potential allies. By forming alliances with affranchi slaveholders, the French crown hoped to preserve the plantations that provided so much wealth to the French economy. Sonthonax was well known for his liberal views and his sympathy for people of color. It was hoped that he would be able to gain affranchi support and pacify both the white colonists and the restless slaves.

But Sonthonax had other ideas. A Freemason who believed in universal brotherhood and the inalienable rights of man, Sonthonax was also a member of *Les amis des noirs* (the Friends of the Blacks), an anti-slavery society. Despite fierce opposition from white colonists, he fought tirelessly for the rights of the affranchis. With the aid of French soldiers, he was able to simultaneously contain the slave uprising to Saint-Domingue's north and to expel radical whites who were seeking independence from France. While France's Freemasons tended to be anticlerical, abolitionist, and critical of royalty, Saint-Domingue's Masonic lodges—white and colored alike—were generally pro-royalist and fiercely pro-slavery. The ardent if somewhat naive Sonthonax quickly learned this lesson and came to despise Saint-Domingue's slaveholders, be they white or mulatto.

In February 1793, France declared war on Britain; later that month Louis XVI was executed and France became the French Republic. Sonthonax saw this as a perfect opportunity to bring the Universal Rights of Man to Saint-Domingue. Faced with the threat of invasion from British troops, as well as Spanish forces on the eastern half of the island, he decided to arm any slave who would fight for France in exchange for their freedom and the freedom of their families. On August 29, 1793, he made this announcement, tearfully announcing before a crowd that he had "a white skin but the soul of a black man." When rumors spread that he had later retracted this declaration, he had a broadside printed in which he declared: "I will support until death the civil rights and the independence of those with mixed blood, of Africans and the descendants of Africans, and that if I were to be pounded into mortar I would never be so low as to retract the proclamation of August 29."[5]

Sonthonax's move was radical, unexpected, and extremely controversial; in 1795 he was called back to France to stand trial for treason. Yet it had the desired effect. The affranchis realized that they would lose whatever rights they had gained should Saint-Domingue fall to the Spanish or English. More important, it gained for France the support of Toussaint L'Ouverture, the brilliant black general who had been fighting for the Spanish. By 1796 the Spanish and British forces had been driven from the island, and Sonthonax had been sent back to Saint-Domingue as its representative.

For Sonthonax, this must have seemed like a triumphant return. Alongside L'Ouverture, his fellow Freemason, he hoped once and for all to liberate the blacks from their oppressors, be they Frenchmen or affranchis. From there he might even spread the gospel of freedom and universal brotherhood to other slaveholding colonies in the Americas. In August 1797, Sonthonax and L'Ouverture had a tense conversation in which Sonthonax recommended slaughtering all the whites on the Saint-Domingue. When L'Ouverture protested "but you are white yourself!" Sonthonax clarified his request to include only those whites who were "enemies of freedom." Realizing that this would only trigger yet more bloodshed, L'Ouverture refused. Ultimately L'Ouverture arranged for Sonthonax to leave Saint-Domingue as one of its elected representatives. When Sonthonax hesitated, L'Ouverture put him under armed escort, then placed him and his family on a ship bound for France on August 24, 1797.

Despite his best efforts, L'Ouverture's efforts at compromise and brotherhood proved unsuccessful. Betrayed by Napoleon's forces, he died in a French dungeon. L'Ouverture's successor and fellow Freemason, Jean-Jacques Dessalines, was more sympathetic to Sonthonax's original idea. After winning control of the colony, he made sure that no colonists were left to threaten his rule. If L'Ouverture hesitated to reward cruelty with cruelty, Dessalines had no such scruples. Contemporary accounts paint a grim picture of Dessalines's revenge:

> General Dessalines had a muster of the white inhabitants then remaining in the place which amounted to almost 450 men, women, and children. When they had collected together he gave orders for their property of every description to be taken from them, and then instantly put to death. In the course of three days 308 were murdered, the remainder have been hid away in different places. The strictest search was made for them and some few found, when they instantly shared the same fate. . . . I assure you that it is horrid to view the streets in different places stained with the Blood of these

unfortunate people, whose bodies are now left exposed to view by the river and sea side. In hauling the seine the evening we came to our anchor several bodies got entangled in it, in fact such scenes of cruelty and devastation have been committed as is impossible to imagine or my pen describe.[6]

Later Haitians who were uncomfortable with the Catholic Church's ties to the mulatto ruling class organized themselves under the banner of Freemasonry. After the Concordat of 1860, when the Catholic Church finally recognized the Haitian government, Catholic clergy returned to Haiti (see chapter 5). But the Catholic clergy at this time were almost exclusively foreigners, drawn from France and taking orders from Rome. The mulatto elite had no problem with this. Since colonial days they had looked to Europe for inspiration; they were happy to put their spiritual needs (and their children's education) in the hands of Frenchmen.

Others, however, were less comfortable with this situation. Louis Joseph Janvier (1855–1911) saw this as a plot to gain political and religious dominance over Haiti. The son of a prosperous Protestant merchant, Janvier was a brilliant scholar; a medical doctor, he had also earned degrees in law, administration, economics, finance, and diplomacy. He was also a dedicated Freemason who believed Catholicism was as foolish and detrimental as the Vodou cults it sought to eradicate. Following the lead of other anticlerical French Freemasons, Janvier favored a government-controlled Protestantism that preached thrift, self-reliance, and personal initiative. Once the folly of carnivals, saint veneration, and other relics of Catholicism could be uprooted from Haiti, Janvier believed Haiti would turn away from its Vodou superstitions and embrace a more practical faith. His writings such as *Haïti aux Haïtiens* and *L'Egalité des Races* inspired many Haitian Freemasons and "ultranationalists," despite the fact that Janvier spent most of his adult life in France.

Much as they had crusaded against Vodou, Haiti's Catholic clergy launched periodic attacks against Freemasonry. In 1884, Masonic posters proclaiming Haiti *"A bas le Grand Maître de l'Ordre"* (under the Grand Master of the order) appeared throughout the capital. This led Port-au-Prince's archbishop to launch voluble attacks against Freemasonry. These soon ceased when it was pointed out that Lysius Salomon, Haiti's president, was the Grand Protector of the order and all of his cabinet members were Freemasons.[7] Ultimately, the Catholic Church came to the same sort of understanding with Haiti's Freemasons as it had with its Vodouisants. The Church confined its attacks to periodic sermons from the pulpit and the Freemasons kept their anticlerical feelings in their lodges. So long as things did not boil over into open violence, everyone was more or less content.

Freemasonry and Vodou

Freemasonry's role in political affairs has been widely (if often sensationally) studied, but it has received less attention for its influence on modern religious movements. Joseph Smith, Brigham Young, and other early Latter-day Saints were high-ranking Freemasons; more than a few observers have noted Masonic influences on Mormon ritual and practice. While Wiccan and Neopagan origin mythology speaks of pre-Christian Europe, many of its rituals come from British Freemasonry; those who read Tarot cards need only look at the High Priestess sitting between the pillars Boaz and Jachin. These pillars are familiar to anyone who has ever taken part in a Masonic initiation; Arthur Edward Waite, designer of the Rider-Waite Tarot deck, was a high-ranking Mason who also wrote *A New Encyclopedia of Freemasonry* and *Secret Tradition in Freemasonry*.

Masonry has had a particularly strong influence on Haitian folk practices. Houngans and mambos refer to Bondye (God) as "Gran Mèt" (Great Master), a Masonic title. The Eye of Providence, or all-seeing eye in the pyramid—found on the American dollar bill—is associated with Freemasonry and is prominently displayed in many peristyles; the *minokan* vévé used to invoke all the lwa is the crossed compass and square, which is a universal symbol of Masonry. Ghede's coffin, skull and crossbones, and shovel could be seen as images of death; those who are familiar with Masonic imagery will also recognize them as potent symbols of rebirth and resurrection. According to Mambo Azan Taye (Edeline St.-Amand) of Jacmel, Haiti, and Brooklyn, New York, "All of the lwa are Masons."[8]

But perhaps the most important influence of Freemasonry on Vodou can be seen in the rite that has come to define Vodou for many: the kanzo (initiation) ceremony by which one becomes a houngan or mambo.

The Kanzo and Freemasonry

For most of Haiti's history, a houngan or mambo didn't need to worry about whether their initiation would be recognized throughout the island. Their entire world might be only twenty miles in each direction; they might die without ever seeing a town of more than a few hundred people. They served their spirits in the ways they were taught by their families. When they couldn't find a particular item for wanga they learned to make do with another. Their relationship with their family spirits grew and changed as they and their descendents grew and changed. There was no country-wide organization that licensed Vodou clergy: initiations tended to be smaller family affairs rather than today's elaborate kanzo ceremony.

These initiatory practices can be seen in Vodu Cubano and Vodu Dominicano, which were established by Haitian migrant workers in the early nineteenth century. We also see them in many of the more rural regions of Haiti, particularly the north. While many think of the asson/kanzo lineage as the only branch of Vodou, or the most "orthodox" form of Vodou, it is actually a comparative newcomer that became popular in the early twentieth century. At that time the deforestation and ecological blight that has become so problematic in today's Haiti was beginning to take its toll. A larger population made subsistence farming more challenging, especially as inheritances resulted in ever-smaller plots of land. An increasing class of landless peasants found their way to Port-au-Prince and other urban centers, where they fought for scarce jobs and struggled to maintain contact with their ancestral traditions.

About this time a royal ancestral lineage that had been preserved from Dahomey began initiating people who were not part of the royal bloodline. We do not know the first houngan to make this break with tradition. He was almost certainly literate, possibly an intellectual forefather of the Noiristes (black nationalist groups). We know that he was also a Freemason, as there are elements of the kanzo that come from Masonic ritual. The handshakes exchanged by initiates are directly paralleled by the "grips" used by Freemasons to identify a brother in the craft; the oaths that are sworn in the *djevo* (initiatory chamber) are nearly identical to the "blood oaths" taken by a Mason. At the culmination of this ceremony, houngans and mambos received the asson, the beaded gourd that was used by the priest-kings in Dahomey to serve Loko.

Undoubtedly our unknown houngan's decision was controversial, but in hindsight it was the right one. Away from their ancestral homes, this new urban working class could reclaim their heritage and connection with the spirits. This initiation became very popular in Port-au-Prince and its environs. Instead of the *kwa-kwas* (rattles) that were used on the rest of the island, these houngans and mambos used elaborately beaded assons. To determine whether a stranger was properly initiated, they could rely on the grips and passwords. As with many other Haitian art and cultural forms, European forms and rituals were grafted onto African roots. Africa was no stranger to initiatory rites of passage or secret societies. While specific details had been lost to time and the Middle Passage, the rituals were not forgotten by the slaves or their descendents. Lacking the specifics, they drew from what they had available to recreate something that met their needs and fulfilled their desire for roots in a rapidly changing world.

During the 1915–1934 American occupation of Haiti and afterward, a growing number of scholars became interested in Haitian traditional religions. They tended to focus on the asson lineage for a number of reasons. Port-au-Prince was more accessible to foreigners traveling by boat than the rugged mountain regions. In rural Haiti spiritual practices were largely a family or village affair. Since the revolution, the Haitian interior has been a place people went to escape from government interference, press gangs, and tax collectors. They were suspicious of strangers and for good reason. In Port-au-Prince the scholars could find clergy who were willing to talk with strangers; if they were particularly dedicated, like Maya Deren, they could even become initiates themselves. There were scholars who studied the rural regions of Haiti: Harold Courlander (1908–1996) did some work on this, and Katherine Dunham (1909–2006) documented a non-asson lineage initiation in her book titled *Island Possessed*.[9] But they were exceptions; for the most part scholarly interest focused on Port-au-Prince and urban Haiti.

In time many seekers came to see what had been described in scholarly journals as "real Vodou" and assumed that anything deviating from those descriptions must somehow be wrong or fraudulent. This was further complicated by a few foreign initiates who decided that the asson lineage was the One True Way of doing Vodou. At worst this leads to the sad spectacle of upper-middle-class foreigners telling Haitians that their family traditions are "bogus" and "phony." At best it privileges one stream of Haitian folk religion—and not even one of the oldest ones—over all others.

While the asson lineage of Vodou was unquestionably influenced by Freemasonry, its primary focus is on the brotherhood of the société rather than on the brotherhood of man. The guidance of one's spiritual leader and the support of one's spiritual family are emphasized; their love and respect is cherished and sought. The rest of the world can think and do as it will; you are inside, and they are out. One does not gain access to the initiatory chamber or société without temwen from someone known and trusted to the société's leaders. One does not expect admittance to a stranger's djevo, nor do they volunteer to *salwe* (salute) the lwa at a stranger's fet. (Indeed, getting possessed at a stranger's party is a social faux pas that implies either that you don't have proper control over your spirits or that you are seeking undeserved attention.) Vodouisants realize that gestures and passwords can be used to affirm a community; but they cannot be used to create community where none exists.

The Lessons of Freemasonry

Since the advent of the Internet many people have decided that "information is free" and secrecy is a fascist concept. There definitely are downsides to secrecy: Abuse survivors are all too familiar with the dark side of "don't tell anybody about this," while governments frequently use "national security" as an excuse to suppress inconvenient or embarrassing data. But there are also reasons why French author and magician Eliphas Levi said that to attain the powers of the Magus one had "to know, to will, to dare, and to keep silence."

You wouldn't discuss the intimate details of your sex life with strangers: if you do, you probably use a relatively anonymous forum such as "A Naughty Nurse's Blog" or "Confessions of a Middle-Aged Lothario." (Those who have been too public in their erotic confessions have frequently found themselves facing the wrath of former lovers, not to mention the unwanted attention of stalkers and predators!) This is because you value your privacy. You don't treat your credit card numbers or bank account information as public information. You understand that they could be misused by people who want to exploit you. The Internet age has also taught us that information is power, and that there are people who will abuse that power if given a chance.

Instead of sharing the details of your life with everyone who asks, you may wish to consider using some discretion. The Internet has also given us many tools for anonymity. When discussing controversial political views, alternative religious beliefs, or other things that might be misunderstood or used against you, we can use an alias. "Christian

Rosenkreuz," founder of the Rosicrucian Order, had no problem sharing his ideas pseudonymously. Although we still don't know exactly who wrote *Chymical Marriage,* we know that its author inspired generations of Rosicrucians and Illuminati.

You may feel uncomfortable about being forced to keep your private life and your professional life separate; it may feel as though you are being censored. Remember that freedom of expression is a luxury. If you cannot afford to be a public crusader for marijuana legalization, polyamory, communism, or whatever other cause you espouse, you will need to find other ways to express your support.

Many anti-Masonic critics claim lodges are hotbeds of cronyism, where members use their Masonic connections for political influence and business dealings. Those who are looking to improve their standing in life might see this as an asset rather than a liability. What sort of networking opportunities do your favored organizations offer? If the members of your magical order are marginally employed and chronically broke, then what is their magic doing for them—or for you?

Today many Masons join not to learn mystical secrets but because it gives them a chance to meet successful people and advance their careers. You may consider joining the Masons (or a similar organization) for that purpose. If you think, "The Masons would never let me join! I'm far too alternative for their tastes!" you may want to stop and think about that as well. If you're so out of the mainstream that your local Masons wouldn't let you join their lodge, what makes you think they would offer you a job? You may laugh at the stodgy businessmen with their polyester suits and comb-over hairdos, but when you need their assistance in getting ahead, don't be surprised if they return the favor and laugh right back.

ABOUT THE COLOR PLATES

The color plates that follow represent images of Legba, Damballah, Agwe, Philomena, Zaka, Ogun, and Ghede from various shrines and Vodou temples. They may provide you with inspiration for your own service to the lwa on a grand scale or in a small corner of your home.

Plate 1. A statue of St. Lazarus, a representation of Legba, shown in the author's home shrine. This shrine includes many offerings given to Legba in exchange for services he has provided.

Plate 2. Shrines need not be large or ornate. This altar to Legba is constructed from an old cigar box. Courtesy of Naufragio Bella, naufragiobella.wordpress.com.

Plate 3. St. Patrick, a representation of Damballah, on the wall of Société la Belle Venus No. 2, Brooklyn, New York.

Plate 4. An altar to Agwe constructed by Dee Dee Snook of the Universal Temple of Spirits, a celebratory, possession-based group; http://globalspirits.org.

Plate 5. St. Ulrique, a representation of Met Agwe, on the wall of Société la Belle Venus No. 2, Brooklyn, New York.

Plate 6. Philomena statue, from the author's collection. This statue is over fifty years old and belonged to an Italian American woman who put her in storage after St. Philomena was removed from the official church calendar.

Plate 7. An altar to Zaka by Mambo Mariah, Universal Spiritualist and Altarista, Studio Ashe, www.studio-ashe.com

Plate 8. St. Isadore, a frequent representation of Zaka, on the wall of Société la Belle Venus No. 2, Brooklyn, New York.

Plate 9. Front of Ogun spirit box (featuring an Ogun vévé) by Mambo Mariah, Universal Spiritualist and Altarista, Studio Ashe, www.studio-ashe.com

Plate 10. Inside Mambo Mariah's Ogun spirit box is a representation of Ogun in his role as ironworker. Courtesy of Studio Ashe, www.studio-ashe.com

Plate 11. Back of Ogun spirit box: locomotives ("iron horses") are often connected to Ogun because of their enormous power and because they run on iron rails. Courtesy of Studio Ashe, www.studio-ashe.com

Plate 12. A Ghede altar created by Mambo Vye Zo Komande (Pat Scheu) of Sosyete du Marche (www.sosyetedumarche.com), a Vodou temple located in Philadelphia, Pennsylvania.

Plate 13. Harvey DelCruccio, the author's house Ghede. Ghede, the jester, is the foul-mouthed spirit of death, lust, and inappropriate behavior who can help you hit the jackpot.

Plate 14. Ancestor altar by Melissa Raquel, Skeleton Key Curio Shop, http://skeletonkeycurio.tripod.com.

Plate 15. Another Ghede altar from Mambo Vye Zo Komande. Mambo Vye Zo knows the way to Ghede's heart: her altar features his favorite colors (purple and black), along with large quantities of food and alcohol.

PART THREE

✳

The Lwa

YOU CAN HAVE VODOU without drums, without temples, without initiates—but you can't have Vodou without the lwa. The lwa can be intercessors, protectors, friends, confidants, and lovers, as familiar to their devotees as their next-door neighbors. Indeed, the word *Vodou* is generally used by outsiders to the faith: Haitian practitioners most commonly refer to the tradition as *sevis lwa,* or "service to the lwa."

If you are used to treating the deities like "archetypes," "god-forms," or other fancy words that mean "imaginary friends," you may find the lwa disturbing in their immediacy and in their concrete demands. The lwa are independent intelligences and behave accordingly—which is why they are both powerful and potentially dangerous. If treated with respect, they can bring great rewards; but if treated casually or disrespectfully, they can wreak havoc. This warning is intended to inspire healthy caution, not fear. Anything that has the capacity to change your life for the better can also change it for the worse. By understanding that, you can take proper precautions and approach the lwa with a healthy respect.

7

Papa Legba
The Old Man at the Crossroads

Bringer of Opportunity

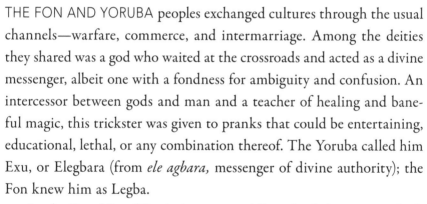

THE FON AND YORUBA peoples exchanged cultures through the usual channels—warfare, commerce, and intermarriage. Among the deities they shared was a god who waited at the crossroads and acted as a divine messenger, albeit one with a fondness for ambiguity and confusion. An intercessor between gods and man and a teacher of healing and baneful magic, this trickster was given to pranks that could be entertaining, educational, lethal, or any combination thereof. The Yoruba called him Exu, or Elegbara (from *ele agbara,* messenger of divine authority); the Fon knew him as Legba.

In the Republic of Benin in western Africa, Legba's statue—which generally features a large, erect, and prominently displayed penis—stands guard at many doorways and village gates. During ceremonies in his honor, dancers wear palm frond skirts in which are hidden wooden phalluses of from ten to eighteen inches (25 to 45 centimeters) long. When Legba comes in possession, he uses that phallus to imitate sexual intercourse with nearby females.[1] Some tell of how Legba became chief of the gods through his ability to simultaneously play a drum, a gong, a bell, and a flute. Others describe his business acumen: he (and later his devotees) made charms to cause disease, then turned a hefty profit selling charms to cure the sickness they had caused![2]

Many Afro-Caribbean traditions see this crossroads trickster as a lively, mischievous young boy, such as Cuba's Ellegua and Brazil's Exu. By contrast, Papa Legba, Haiti's spirit of the crossroads, is a tattered old man dressed in rags. Whereas Ellegua and Exu dance suggestively, Legba leans on his cane and limps down *la gran chemin,* the eternal road that is the sun's daily arc and the pathway between the mortal and divine worlds; Vodouisants sing of him "limping along" and of his "old, old bones."

But although Legba may appear to be a feeble old man, Vodouisants believe that none of the lwa can "come down" to this world without his assistance. He is the gatekeeper and the catalyst: he stands in every time and every place where two ways are joined. Vodouisants believe that Legba carries blessings and curses in the straw *makout* (gunnysack) that he carries over his shoulder, and that his walking stick stretches from the depths to the heavens. He is the first lwa saluted in a Vodou ceremony; every wanga must begin with an offering to Legba if it is to succeed.

Legba is most often represented by images of St. Lazarus, the leprous lame beggar. Other staff-carrying saints have been pressed into service, notably St. Jude, St. Roch, and St. Christopher. St. Anthony, "finder of lost things," has been used as a representation of Legba, and so has St. Peter, "keeper of the Keys of Heaven." In our house, Legba's colors are yellow and white; other houses use red and white.

Legba is an easygoing and generally benevolent lwa; Vodouisants hail him as Atibon Legba, or "Good Old Legba." For a few drops of salt water he will open the way for Met Agwe (chapter 9); a sprinkling of Florida Water will suffice for Danto (chapter 13); and a libation of rum will persuade him to let Ogou (chapter 12) come down. But Vodouisants also know that Legba can bring bad luck as well as good; he can either open the way or put insurmountable obstacles in your path. Those who are wise will pay extra attention to this humble and unassuming spirit; they will soon find their kindness richly rewarded.

Working with Legba

Even though Haitian Vodouisants recognize Legba's power and importance, he is not one of the more popular lwa. In Haiti, Legba does not receive the attention lavished on Freda, nor is he feted with enormous parties the way Ogou and Ghede are. Outside Haiti, however, Legba has become a very well-known and loved spirit. In 1986, the group Talking Heads sang to "Papa Legba" on its *True Stories* CD, while William Gibson's cyberpunk classic novel *Count Zero* gave Legba a leading role. Marvel Comics introduced Legba as a member of The Eternals in 2008, and Damien Duffy and John Jennings gave us a world in which Legba's benign and malevolent sides had split apart in *The Hole: Consumer Culture, Volume 1.*

Many foreign Vodouisants (including the author) first encounter Legba on their journey into Vodou. This is not surprising. Legba is more open to strangers than some of the other, more clannish lwa. If you are a newcomer to Vodou, you will do well to make Legba's acquaintance. You can give him the bare minimum required for his services and get acceptable results; Legba will do his job if he is paid the required wage. But if you want him to give you extra assistance and introduce you to other lwa, you will find that added effort leads to added reward. This lesson also applies to the business world: cultivating good relations with the person at the reception desk can be more useful than fawning over the head of the corporation.

As in Benin, Haitian shrines to Legba are often kept near the doorway or gate. If you can place your Legba near your door, that is ideal, but if not, don't worry: Legba will be content with just about any space to rest his weary bones. A yellow cloth on your floor and a small St. Lazarus image will suffice. We serve Legba on Monday, but he can be honored on any day. Among his favored offerings are peanuts, roasted corn, cane syrup or molasses, and pipe tobacco. If you want to "heat up" your Legba and speed a situation along, you might sprinkle Legba's food liberally with cayenne pepper. To "sweeten" him and improve your luck, you might give him cane syrup or other sweet foods.

Because of Legba's love of ambiguity, it is difficult to give specific instructions for working with him. As you develop a relationship with him, he will likely ask you for specific items that may appear to be absurd. (The usual disclaimer applies: don't give your spirits anything that violates applicable laws, and don't be afraid to bargain or to say, "No, Papa, I can't do that for you! Here is what I *can* give you.") Your relationship with Legba is certain to be unique and at times puzzling. We've happily provided our Legba with Tiki mugs and bobble-headed dogs ("But not Chihuahuas! Those things are too noisy!"). In return, he has looked after us and provided us with numerous material and spiritual opportunities. Mambo Zetwal Kleye (Kathy Latzoni) points out that Legba's seemingly random antics often conceal multiple layers of meaning: "I've received messages from Legba and six months later everything would fall into place, like the punch line to some elaborate shaggy dog story. Legba is one of the old, old lwa; his communications aren't always in our time frame."[3]

Legba is more easygoing than his Cuban and Brazilian cousins, but that doesn't mean he has lost his sense of humor or his love of a prank. When you ask Legba for a blessing, it's likely to arrive from unexpected quarters. Look for elaborate puns, improbable "coincidences," and general weirdness. When working with Legba, the old cliché applies: expect the unexpected. A sense of humor and an ability to adapt to changing situations will help greatly.

Finally, when asking Legba for something, make sure you really want it. If you put Legba in motion and ask him to make changes in your life, he will make those changes—even if he has to drag you along like a screaming toddler! In my practice, I've found that many people want to complain about their problems, but they don't really want to do anything about them and indeed would have difficulty adjusting to life without their problems. I've also met many people who thought they were pursuing their dream while they were really pursuing someone else's. ("Of course I've always wanted to be a doctor. We have six generations of doctors in our family!") Legba will guide you down the path you choose. Take responsibility for your life and choose wisely.

A Clean Start with Legba

When you are trying to get yourself out of a financial mess (or into a financial windfall), it helps to first straighten out your surroundings. Getting your workplace and home organized gives you better access to necessary paperwork. It also provides a more restful environment and helps keep away negativity. The old claim that "Cleanliness is next to godliness" has some basis in fact: benevolent spirits generally favor well-scrubbed and orderly places, while malevolent entities favor corruption, decay, and clutter.

This ritual can be done in your workplace; you can use this to straighten out your store, your office, your employee locker—wherever you earn your daily bread. If you work from home, you can do this ritual as a housecleaning; in fact, it would probably be good if you did this both at home and at work.

Light a white candle. A simple emergency candle, also known as a Sabbath candle, is sufficient. As you do, ask Legba to light your way so that you stay on the right path and avoid blind alleys and wrong turns. Purify your space by whatever means you usually use: calling the quarters, fumigating with sage or frankincense, sprinkling holy water, saying the Rosary, and so on. Purifications are a very important step in any Vodou working—and should be part of any ceremony that involves calling on the spirit world!

If you are doing this at your job, you may not be able to light a candle, burn incense, or even say vocal prayers. In that case, get a St. Lazarus Holy Card and place it in your workplace. Sprinkle a few drops of water discreetly on the ground and silently ask Legba for his assistance and guidance.

Now clean as thoroughly as you can, starting at the back and working toward the front. Make sure the space is thoroughly clean and the dust swept into a neat pile near the door. As you are sweeping, make a mental inventory of all the things you want to leave behind in your professional and personal life—bad habits you want to break, weaknesses and failings that hold you back, and so on. There's no better time than now to literally and figuratively "make a clean sweep."

Continue thinking of all those problems as you sweep them up into a brown paper bag and close it. You are now going to take that dust and those problems to your nearest crossroads. It's best if the crossroads is near a house of worship or some place of natural beauty; try to avoid a crossroads near a graveyard, funeral home, or hospital. It's also best if the crossroads is both safe and relatively quiet, since you will need a moment or two undisturbed. Along with the dust, you are going to bring some peanuts, a banana, some toasted corn, a little bit of pocket change, and a bottle of cane syrup.

Empty the bag of dust on the side of the road by the crossroads. As you do, feel all the burdens and obstacles that you swept into that bag falling away from you; you are going to meet Legba, so you no longer need or want them. They are part of your old path; they are from where you have been, not where you are going. (Take the bag away and dispose of it in the nearest trash receptacle; don't take it back to your house. Legba doesn't mind you dumping your troubles at his crossroads, but he would prefer that you take your litter with you when you leave.)

Cross the street. As you cross, you are walking away from the detritus of your past. When you reach the other side, you will be ready to give Legba his offering. Leave the toasted corn, peanuts, banana, and pocket change by the roadside. Thank Legba for his help and tell him that you would like a closer relationship with him from now on. Spend a little time with Legba: listen to any advice he may give or just take the opportunity to reflect on where you are. When you are finished, take out your bottle of cane syrup and pour a little on the ground.

Now return to your workplace. Along the way, pour out little dribbles of cane syrup whenever you get a chance. If you are driving, you can stop a few times on the way and leave your mark in rest stops, parking lots, and so forth. This will leave a sweet trail for Legba to find his way to your house and bring good fortune along with him. Be on the lookout for unusual omens, strange events, or other "signs" that suggest Legba has accepted your offering and is trying to send you a message.

When you get to your workplace, pour what is left of the corn syrup out onto your lawn. Welcome Legba—and new opportunities—into your life. What happens afterward is entirely up to you. You have left your old habits behind, but that doesn't mean you can't pick them up again if you're not careful. Once you've cleaned house, you need to stay on top of things lest they degenerate again.

Git-R-Done with Legba

Any freelancer knows the special joy of waiting for contracts and checks. Your creditors are never as patient and slow-moving as the folks who owe you money, or the guy who is just waiting to hire you as soon as he gets approval from the rest of the committee. When you have bills that just won't wait, and laggard clients who won't get off the stick and pay you, you can call on Legba for help. He can remove the obstacles standing between you and your money, and light a fire under those who are hesitant about doing the right thing.

For this ritual you will need some peanuts, cayenne pepper, and roasted corn. (I have it on good authority that roasted corn snacks or even cornflakes will do.) You will also need a sheet of plain unlined paper, some red ribbon, a red pen that you have never used, seven stickpins (preferably with red pinheads), a red seven-day candle, and a shot glass full of white rum to which you have added a few drops of hot sauce.

Light the red seven-day candle and ask Legba to come to your aid. Now sprinkle the cayenne pepper liberally on the roasted corn and peanuts. As you do, the air becomes hotter; feel Legba coming toward you like a far-off forest fire. Offer the corn, peanuts, and spiced rum to Legba; explain your problem and thank him for his help.

Draw Legba's vévé (pictured at the beginning of this chapter) on the white paper using the red pen. As you do, imagine the lines glowing like embers. By creating this symbol, you are calling Legba into this time and space. When the vévé is finished, sign your name at the top of the page. At the bottom of the page write the name of the person, people, or business you wish to influence.

Fold the paper in half so that your name is above the target's name. Now that you are on top of the target, you are in a dominant position over them. Tell them what they have to do, and order them to get to it.

Now stick the first pin in the folded paper, in the right top corner. Say, "I order this in the name of Atibon Legba that he may look upon me with kindness."

Stick the second pin in the paper, next to the first. Say, "I order this in the name of Gran Chemin, the great road, that this quest may reach its end."

As you insert the third pin, say, "I order this in the name of Legba Avadra the wanderer, that he may find what should be mine."

The fourth pin, "I order this in the name of Vye Vye Legba the Old Man, that he may take pity upon his grandchild and grant me what should be mine."

The fifth pin, "I ask this in the name of Legba Kay, Legba of the House, that we may harvest what we have sown."

The sixth pin, "I order this in the name of Legba Do Miwo, Legba behind the mirror, that he may bring to light what is hidden from me."

The seventh and final pin, "I ask this in the name of Legba Met Carrefour, Legba master of the crossroads, that he may lead [insert name here] on the path I desire."

Wrap the now thoroughly pinned paper in red ribbon. As you do, feel Legba's energy filling the paper. In binding this charm, you are binding your target. The paths that they have taken to avoid you are now closed; the only option open to them is to do your bidding and grant you that which you deserve. They have no more excuses; all that is left for them is to do what they should already have done.

Sprinkle the wrapped paper with cayenne pepper. As you do, imagine that Legba is "lighting a fire" underneath them. They will feel restless and out of sorts until they move; the longer they wait, the more pronounced this discomfort will become. (If you feel guilty about this, consider all the hardship their inaction has caused you.) Feel the heat blazing from the charm. You are in the presence of Legba as he truly is; you are face to face with the power behind his unassuming façade. This presence is now working for you to move things along and burning to ashes any obstacle that would stand in your way.

If you already have a Legba shrine, place this charm on that shrine; keep it in a box or pouch or otherwise hidden from prying eyes. Talk to this charm and to Legba every day until the desired outcome is reached. Complain to the charm; give it more cayenne pepper and encourage Legba to redouble his efforts in persuading your target. In the meantime reward him with jalapeño jelly, red-hot cinnamon balls, or similar sweet/spicy offerings. This will keep him happy while ensuring he stays hot and working on your case.

You may notice heightened energy bordering on mania during this time. Since your name is on the charm, you are likely to absorb some of Legba's essence as he works. Staying in touch with Legba will help to ensure that this force is grounded and channeled in a positive and productive way. When the target finally gives in, be sure to reward Legba well for his efforts.

Perusing the Want Ads with Legba

When you're unemployed, hunting for work can become its own special kind of torment. Joblessness isn't just a threat to your finances, it's a blow to your self-esteem. After spending weeks or months sending out resumes without a nibble, you can start thinking of yourself as unworthy, unqualified, and utterly useless. If you find yourself falling into this kind of spiral, you can call on Legba. When you ask him for work, he will happily guide you toward new opportunities.

To perform this spell you will need your local newspaper(s). Look through the classifieds sections and circle in red pen anything that you find intriguing. Next go through the entire paper and circle any story or advertisement that mentions a company where you might like to work or an industry that interests you. You can use multiple newspapers for this. You are also encouraged to include printouts of any online job offer that strikes your fancy. When you are finished, cut out every item that you have circled in red ink and put them in a small, white, oven-safe ceramic baking dish (a small soufflé dish is the ideal size). If you need to cut the printouts into smaller pieces to make sure they all fit, don't worry about it; Legba enjoys unscrambling puzzles and will have no difficulty interpreting your request.

Draw Legba's vévé on a sheet of brown grocery bag paper, using the red pen that you used before. Place it on top of a yellow or red cloth. Get a cake pan large enough for the smaller ceramic dish to fit easily inside it. Fill the pan approximately one-third full of water so that the smaller dish is surrounded; add a few drops of cane syrup or molasses. Place the pan, dish, and water atop the vévé. Then place a yellow seven-day candle in the pan.

Light the candle. Ask Bondye, the Highest Power, to look after you and yours, and to grant you an audience with Legba. (Legba may be the opener of the gate, but like all the other lwa, he can only act "as God wills.") Now take a few drops of water from the pan and sprinkle them on the ground. As you do, feel Papa Legba coming to greet you. You are calling on Atibon Legba (Good Old Legba), one of Legba's most merciful and benevolent aspects. He is old and ragged, but his eyes twinkle with life and his step is surprisingly spry as he comes toward you on his crutch.

Tell your problems to Papa Legba. Explain to him how you have been hunting for work. Tell him how much you need a job and how many people are relying on you. Be honest with him and don't hold anything back. Papa Legba has walked down many roads and knows what it's like to be poor and hungry and wandering with no place to go. He will gladly help you find a job to call your own.

In exchange for his help, offer him a fire to warm his old bones; ignite the newspaper clippings and shredded printouts. (First, make sure that you are far enough away from anything flammable, such as curtains, bookshelves, or the like.) As you watch the paper burn, feel the warmth flowing through you and through Legba; both of you stand silently absorbing its glow. As the papers crackle into dust, their message vanishes in this world and is conveyed to the land *sonde miroir* (behind the mirror), the place where Legba reigns, the place between what is and what was and what is to come.

When the paper has finished burning, take it to a crossroads and scatter it to the winds. As you do so, ask Legba to bring job opportunities your way. Next return home by the same way that you came. Allow the seven-day candle to burn out, then pour out the water on your doorstep or in your front yard.

Needless to say, you should accompany this spell with the usual mundane steps such as sending out resumes, networking with friends, and looking for Help Wanted signs. Legba likes to surprise you with unexpected blessings, but you have to be open to receiving them. And, as always, be sure to give Legba his due when he brings you a job.

8

Damballah

The Great Serpent

Financial Solvency and Spiritual Elevation

IN THE WESTERN WORLD, snakes have received a bad rap. In Christian mythology a serpent talks Eve into eating the forbidden fruit, thereby bringing death and suffering to her and her descendents. Each year many snakes are killed by frightened people, even though the majority of snakes are harmless to humans and most venomous snakes would rather avoid humans than bite them.

By contrast, Fon farmers have long paid tribute to Da, the great white python who brought the rain and ensured abundant crops. They knew that one bad harvest could (and did) lead to widespread famine. Devotees of Da believed that he had many serpent children and so avoided killing any snake. Those who willfully killed a python could be sentenced to death, and a python that died of natural causes was given a public burial.[1] Although European colonists and explorers mocked these traditions as superstition or devil worship, defending the snakes was perfectly sensible. Rodents eat stored food—and snakes eat rats and mice. By allowing Da's children into their granaries and storehouses, the snakes protected the supply from the rodent scavengers.

The Fon believed the universe was a sphere that resembled the two halves of a calabash gourd; the horizon marked the line between the top and bottom halves. This sphere floated within another larger sphere that was filled with water. In the beginning of time Da coiled himself about the earth and gathered it together atop the water, then welded together the spheres and held them in his coils. Were he to loosen his seven thousand coils (thirty-five hundred above the earth in the realm of the gods and thirty-five hundred below in the deep waters), all creation would come to an end. His grip is not stationary; his constant undulations cause the heavenly bodies to move in their orbits, and when they are particularly intense, to engender earthquakes. Wherever Da rested on the earth, mountains arose; the tracks of his movement can be seen in the beds of rivers and streams. Da can be seen in many forms. The most well known is Da-Ayido-Hwedo, who most commonly appears as a rainbow.[2] Many Africans believe the Milky Way is starlight shining off Da's scales.

Various Fon strongmen fought for control of the lucrative slave trade until 1727, when King Agadja of Dahomey conquered the region. In the battle, more than five thousand people were slaughtered; eleven thousand more were sent into slavery. The Dahomey kings then controlled the ports of Allada and Ouidah. Over the next century they would grow wealthy selling their countrymen to European traders. Among their most loyal customers were the French, and so the Rada (from Allada) lwa and Damballah Wedo came to occupy a very prominent place in Saint-Domingue and later in Haitian Vodou.

Damballah is one of the oldest lwa. He is so old that he does not trouble himself with human speech: typically when Damballah comes in possession he is silent, although sometimes he will make a high-pitched whistling noise like a snake hissing. A person possessed by Damballah will fall to the floor and slither on the ground. When Damballah comes, devotees will typically throw a white sheet on the ground so he does not have to slither in the dirt. They will also throw a white sheet over him to protect him from the hot sun and from the gaze of those who are not worthy to behold him. When Damballah arrives outside, the celebrants keep a careful eye on him to make sure he doesn't begin climbing any nearby trees; he has been known to slither like a snake to a high branch, then go away, leaving his *chwal* ("horse" or possessed person) to climb down.

In Africa, Ayida-Hwedo is an aspect of Da; in Haiti she is Damballah's wife, along with Freda, lwa of love, beauty, and luxury. The excellent Wade Davis book (and the execrable Wes Craven movie) paid tribute to their pairing in the title *The Serpent and the Rainbow*. Some houses represent Damballah with images of St. Patrick, since the most commonly available lithograph for St. Patrick features several snakes. Others represent him with images of the white-bearded patriarch Moses, as a token of Damballah's great age. His colors are white (some say white and green), and his feast day is St. Patrick's Day, March 17. Fets held in Damballah's honor also pay tribute to the first houngan, Papa Loko (frequently syncretized with St. Joseph, the father of Jesus). Some say this is because St. Joseph's feast day (March 19) falls very close to St. Patrick's Day; others say that it is because both are among the highest and holiest of the lwa.

Working with Damballah

When you wish to petition Damballah, you must remember that he likes things to be tidy. Make sure the area where you will be doing the working is thoroughly clean. Sweep or vacuum the floors, dust and polish as required, and straighten any clutter. You want the area to be as clean and pure as a cathedral: Damballah is one of the oldest and holiest of the lwa and deserves nothing less. This is actually a good way to begin any spiritual endeavor. Rituals to cleanse and purify your space will be much more effective when combined with a thorough physical cleaning. Stagnant water and rotting food can provide nourishment for undesirable negative entities, and it's far more difficult to get your thoughts in order when you're surrounded by disorder.

When Damballah is being saluted at a fet, the congregation will cap any open containers and put out their cigarettes. If you have a permanent altar to Damballah in your home, avoid drinking or smoking near it. (If that is impossible, you can always create a temporary altar and pack it away when you are finished calling on him.) Needless to say, you should avoid calling on Damballah—or any other lwa—when you are under the influence of alcohol or any other mind-altering substances. (Entheogens are not part of Haitian Vodou practice and should not be used in any spiritual setting without proper guidance and safeguards.) You should also avoid working with Damballah if you are menstruating or if you have an open cut or wound. Damballah does not like the smell of blood. On the rare occasions when he is offered a sacrifice of doves or white chickens, their necks are broken rather than cut; they are also killed outside the peristyle so that no stray drops might offend him.

Considering these demands, you may think Damballah is a difficult or temperamental spirit. Nothing could be further from the truth: once you make his acquaintance, he is one of the most patient and undemanding of the lwa. The things he asks for are things that will be beneficial for you, too. If you're willing to do magic to get money, surely you should be willing to clean your house or refrain from smoking near your altar.

As one of the oldest lwa, Damballah tends to take a long-range view of problems. What seems to be a terrible emergency to you may be no great matter to him. This is not because he lacks compassion but because he knows that things will be fine once the turmoil clears. If you are a parent, you've probably had to convince your children on at least a few occasions that the world wouldn't come to an end if they didn't get their way. Damballah is not afraid to do the same for his children. But also like any parent, Damballah is quick to act when his children are in real danger. Anyone who has ever seen a placid snake strike at its target understands just how fast Damballah can move when action is required.

Whereas many of the other lwa prefer rum, Damballah drinks *sirop d'orgeat,* a sweet almond-flavored syrup. You can find this in many coffee shops; it's used to flavor your almond latte. If you can't find this, you can make simple syrup by boiling a cup of water, then adding a cup of sugar and stirring until it is dissolved. (If you'd like, you can also add almond extract and/or a sprinkling of rose water; the finished syrup will keep in the refrigerator for up to a week.) His favorite perfume is Lotion Pompeia, a French cologne with notes of rose, jasmine, ylang-ylang, iris, lemon, lavender, geranium, and patchouli. Pompeia is available in many botanicas or online, but in a pinch, you can substitute rosewater or orange flower water.

The most common offering made to Damballah is an egg on top of a heap of white flour. The egg is first washed with Lotion Pompeia to make sure it is clean, then placed on the white flour. You can also burn a white candle when you want to call on him. An immaculate white cloth can be used to cover his altar, and inexpensive but clean white china can be used to hold his offerings. You can use an image of St. Patrick or Moses to represent Damballah, or you can use a white snake. (We have a small white jade dragon on top of our Damballah altar and a large albino Burmese python beneath it.) I have found that it is best to keep a Damballah shrine as simple as possible; instead of getting many items for him, give him only a few things he will really like.

Petitioning Damballah for Financial Help in Spiritual Affairs

As much as we may wish to separate spiritual matters from filthy lucre, sometimes even heavenly goals require earthly funding. Every temple needs contractors and laborers; every charity needs donations. (And if you're complaining about the cost of initiation into Vodou, ask some Divinity School students about their student loans sometime.) But how do you put the money together for spiritual things when you are struggling to meet your worldly obligations?

In a situation like this you can rely on Papa Damballah for help. While at times he may seem aloof and unconcerned with humans, he is happy to assist in our spiritual elevation. As a popular *chanté lwa* (song for the spirits) for Damballah says, he leaves tracks wherever he goes. He may not move as quickly as you might like, but he will get you where you need to go—and make powerful, lasting changes in every aspect of your life.

For this spell you will need a glass of water, a clean white saucer, white flour, and a white egg. You will also need a white covered casserole dish. If you can get "snake shed" (ideally from a white or albino snake), that will work particularly well; if not, you can use clean, new white yarn. (There's a difference between a snake shed and snakeskin: the former is sloughed off without harm to the snake.) For the table you will need a clean white cloth and a white seven-day candle. You will need Lotion Pompeia or rose water for cleansing. Finally, you will need an a Damballah vévé that you have drawn yourself in green ink on unlined white paper and another piece of blank paper. If there are other things that you have already gathered in service to Damballah, you can use them as well.

Determine how much your spiritual goal is going to cost. If you don't have a clear estimate, this is the time to get one. Putting together money for detailed plans is much easier than trying to fund idle dreams. You may want to use the "Planning Your Future with General Ogou Badagri" spell (see chapter 12) along with all of the appropriate footwork and research. Also, determine what percentage of your income you can give to that goal. The biblical tithe (10 percent) is a good number to start with, but you may go with a lower or higher amount as your situation requires. Be liberal in what you are willing to put aside: the Divine is generous to those who are generous, and with Damballah's aid you may soon find yourself making back your offering with interest.

Wipe down the surface where you will be working with the Pompeia or rose water. Place the vévé on that surface, then place the white cloth on top of it. Put the glass and saucer on the cloth. Fill the glass with water, then add a few drops of perfume. Place the flour on the saucer and then place the egg on top. Put the candle atop the cloth, along with the white casserole dish and any personal Damballah items you may have.

Sprinkle a few drops of the water on the floor, and ask Legba to open the door so that Papa Damballah may come through. Next, light the candle and offer the egg and water to Damballah. As you do, feel something huge moving toward you. It is white and shining and as massive as mountains as it comes toward you, moving closer until you see its great bright scales. You realize that what you thought might be a glacier or an oncoming avalanche is actually the nose of an enormous white serpent, a snake so vast that its coils encircle the earth and its great green eyes are as large as the sun and the moon. You stand transfixed before him, beyond joy and beyond terror, silent in the pure peace of Damballah.

Stay there silent for a few minutes. Damballah's very presence brings healing and empowerment. When you feel it is time, explain your situation to Damballah. Make a contract promising that you will devote a certain percentage of each paycheck to the spiritual investment you have chosen. Write a promise to that effect, using the pen with which you drew the vévé on the other sheet of paper.

Sign your promise, then roll up the sheet and tie it using snakeskin or white yarn. (The snake shed may be brittle so tie carefully.) As you do, feel Damballah exploring your promise and sealing it. Place the promise in your casserole dish along with the first installment on your payment plan. Ask Damballah to help you faithfully pay your obligations to this promise in a timely manner. Also ask him to provide you with enough to support your family and pay your bills while you are putting this money aside. In return for his help, promise him that each pay period you will give him flour and an egg until your goal is met. Spend some quiet time with Damballah. When you are finished, snuff out the candle with your fingers (don't blow it out) and break down the altar. Wrap the casserole dish in the white cloth and put it away in a clean place where it will not be disturbed.

When you next get paid, put that money aside before you do anything else. Set the table up in the same fashion, sprinkle some water for Legba, then light the candle and show Damballah your offering. Continue doing this until you have amassed enough to pay for your goal. Be on the lookout for gifts or sudden windfalls that will help you reach your dream more quickly. Damballah will often provide favors to those on the right path, particularly those who are developing a personal relationship with him.

Curb Impulse Spending with Damballah

If you want to learn about patience, consider the serpent. A snake will lay motionless for hours or even days, waiting for a meal to cross its path. It does not lash out blindly at shadows, nor does it waste energy on prey that is too small, too large, or outside its strike range. This steady approach has worked marvelously for snakes: we have fossil records of snakes dating back 100 million years.[3]

Contrast that methodical approach with the habits of the impulse shopper—a label that has fit most of us at one time or another. The impulse shoppers wander into a store looking for one particular item—some new socks, let us say. But before they can reach the underwear aisle, they spy some tempting gewgaws beneath a large, brightly colored "33 Percent Off" sign. Casting aside their plans, they buy the latest electronic toy or designer label handbag, then justify their purchase by saying "I saved a hundred dollars" when they actually wasted two hundred dollars on an item that they didn't really need.

When you're shopping and see an attractive, prominently placed item, you may do well to consider another trick used by many snakes—caudal luring. Some snakes will wriggle their tails to attract a victim's attention. A bird spots what looks like a tasty worm, then saunters into range and becomes an easy meal itself. Retail outlets also recognize the value of catching their prey's attention. Goods that produce more profit for retailers are placed at the end of aisles or near cash registers to attract consumer attention; for added impact, enticing sale signs are often added. The next time you're tempted to buy one of these prominently placed items, remember that unfortunate bird.

In our credit-driven culture, it can be hard to resist temptation. When even hedge funds and investment banks are unable to resist buying things they can't afford, how can we as individuals expect to get our spending habits under control? One way is to call on Damballah. He is not given to reckless behavior, nor is he easily distracted. With his assistance, you may find your local shopping mall a less dangerous place.

This ritual will require many of the items used in the previous spell: a glass of water (or sirop d'orgeat), a clean white saucer, white flour and a white egg, along with a white cloth, white seven-day candle, Lotion Pompeia (or rose water), and Damballah's vévé. You will also need a white wallet: if you can't find one, a green or silver wallet will do. It can be made of any material except snakeskin: snakeskin wallets are made by killing and skinning large constrictors! (Again, a snake shed is simply shed, or sloughed off, a live snake without harm to the snake.)

Set up the space as you did in the previous spell; place the wallet on the table as well. Sprinkle some of the water or sirup on the ground and ask Legba to open the way for Papa Damballah. Now light the candle and offer the egg and water/sirop to Damballah. Wait quietly for a few minutes, until you feel the great serpent making his way toward you.

When Damballah has arrived, explain your situation to him. Tell him how your bad spending habits have led you into debt, and ask him to help you mend your ways. Present the white wallet to him: tell him that from now on you will use this whenever you go shopping, so that you will be reminded of him each time you make a purchase. When you are finished, snuff out the candle, dispose of the egg and flour outside, then fold the vévé and put it in the white wallet.

Whenever you want to go shopping (and that includes online shopping), place your credit cards and money in the wallet along with Damballah's vévé. Tell him beforehand what you plan to buy. If it is an expensive item, or one that will require you going into debt, be ready to justify your purchase. (Do you absolutely *have* to have that new extra-large television? Will you enjoy it more than a slightly smaller and cheaper model—or will you find that your favorite programs look and sound just as good on your current TV?)

If you see something that looks irresistible but that wasn't on your shopping list, remember how a snake waits for its meals. Make a written note of the item in question and place it in Damballah's wallet. Go home and prepare another offering for Damballah and ask him if you really should buy this or not. (You may well find that you're no longer interested by the time you get home: just think of how many impulse purchases you regretted as soon as you left the store!) If you find you still want this item a week later, look around to see if you can find a better deal on it or a comparable item.

This will help you to avoid making foolish purchases; if you find it is not enough, you may have a more serious problem. Debtors Anonymous (www.debtorsanonymous.com) can provide you with a community of others who share your addiction and can provide you with support in overcoming it. You may also wish to seek therapy from a licensed counselor. Damballah brings healing to his devotees, but as befits a serpent, he doesn't waste energy. If you are looking for a spectacular and miraculous cure from the heavens, you may well miss the signs pointing you to a good doctor or some other mundane means of dealing with your problem.

Rational Financial Planning with Damballah

As you watch the financial markets convulse and see property values sinking like stones, it's hard not to get caught up in the general anxiety. You may want to liquidate all your investments and hide the money in your mattress. You may stay in an unfulfilling and low-paying job rather than seeking out something more suited to your needs. You may even be tempted to take a chance on shady and possibly illegal schemes out of sheer desperation. These actions may seem perfectly sensible, given the current climate. But are you acting on logical concerns or reacting out of blind terror?

For centuries economists have assumed that the marketplace acted on rational concerns. According to this model, businessmen and consumers make logical, self-interested decisions, weighing costs against benefits to maximize their gains and minimize their losses. Today we have realized that individuals and organizations do not always act based on reason at all; the same blind emotions that lead to stampedes and mob violence come into play in the financial world as well.

To make matters worse, recent trends have favored short-term profits at the expense of sustainability. At one time investors purchased stocks expecting to hold onto them for decades. Fluctuations in the marketplace did not concern them so long as their holdings showed growth over the long haul. A house was a home for you and your family, not an investment that was expected to produce annual gains. Today day traders buy and sell stocks as if they were exchanging sports cards, while the practice of "house flipping"—buying a home, then selling it soon after at an anticipated profit—played a major role in the 2007–08 mortgage meltdown. If you are caught up in that mindset, it's easy to panic at the first sign of trouble—and fall into the trap of buying high and selling low.

Financial success requires an ability to see beyond immediate troubles. This is one of Damballah's particular strengths. He has been around since the days when those pesky fuzzy creatures challenged the dinosaurs for supremacy and won: he knows the difference between a true crisis and a problem that looks horrible but which will soon be resolved. By establishing a relationship with him and calling on his counsel, you will be able to make much better decisions about your future.

If you have a question concerning your future or your investments, petition Damballah on a Thursday evening. Set up a typical table on his behalf: a glass of water or sirup, a candle, a white cloth, an egg, and some flour on a white saucer, his vévé, and so on. (See the preceding spells for more details.) Place any paperwork connected to your question on the table. For example, if you are wondering about your job, you can use a paycheck stub; if you are concerned with your investments, you can use a recent statement.

Sprinkle some water or sirup on the floor as an offering to Legba so he will open the gate. Now light the candle and wait for Papa Damballah to arrive. You will know his presence by the sense of peace and calm that falls over you. Spend a few minutes luxuriating in that calm, letting yourself be blessed by Damballah. Feel him staring at you with his great green eyes; hear the soft even hiss of his breathing as he coils about you and turns your home into a holy place.

Now that you are in a calm and centered place, discuss your concerns with Damballah. Explain your fears and ask for his advice. While he may not answer in words, you will feel in your heart what you should do. If your fears are unjustified, he will take them away; if they are real, he will help you deal with them. Damballah speaks to his children through what Vodouisants call *konesans* (from the French word *connaissance*)—an instinctive deep knowledge of what is to be done. He does not talk using words, but he has no difficulty conveying information to those who ask. You may feel like the message you get is unclear, even illogical; this is not at all uncommon, since the spirits often tell us what we need to know rather than what we expect or wish to hear.

When you are finished, thank Damballah for coming to your aid. Snuff the candle out, then spend a few minutes in quiet contemplation. Now that you have a better idea of what you should do, it's up to you to put Damballah's advice into action. He may show you the way and give you the strength to do what must be done—but you are going to have to follow through on his advice. If you feel frightened or unsure, put your trust in Damballah and know that he will not turn away from those who put their trust in him, nor will he lead them astray.

9

Met Agwe Tawoyo
The Emperor beneath the Waves

Bringer of Diplomacy and Professionalism

THE LAND BENEATH HAITI'S waves is as rugged and mountainous as the terrain above. To the north, under water, lies the dividing line between the North American and Caribbean tectonic plates. The friction between the two has carved the Puerto Rico Trench, an undersea valley whose floor lies beneath eighty-four hundred meters (more than five miles) of water—the deepest point in the Atlantic Ocean. Port-au-Prince's seaport, the Gulf of Gonave, marks the border of yet another ocean trench, the Cayman Trough—the deepest point in the Caribbean Ocean.

Vodou mythology places *Gineh*—ancestral Africa—beneath these deep waters. The ocean is also home to *La Ville aux Camps,* the home of the lwa. *"Chapeau tombe nan la mer"*—"My hat fell into the ocean"—is a Kreyol synonym for trance possession; the sea is seen as a place of great power and great danger.

Not surprisingly, Met Agwe Tawoyo (in French "Agouet-Aroyo"), ruler of the ocean, is one of the most important and powerful of the lwa. A boat representing Agwe's ship, the *Imamou*—and typically marked with its name—can be found in peristyles throughout Haiti. Some say that it brings the lwa from beneath the ocean to our world, and/or that it carries the blessed dead "under the water" to the land of the blessed ancestors. The *yanvalou,* a dance performed for the Rada

110

spirits, is a tribute to Agwe and La Sirene; the rocking motion of the dancers evokes the gentle rhythm of the waves.[1]

Agwe has clear roots in Benin, where the Ewe peoples call him "Agoueh" and the Fon call him "Hu." But as the sea takes in many rivers, so has Agwe drawn from other traditions. Some say his last name suggests that he comes from the port city of Awoyo, where the king of the sea was honored. Others believe it comes from a Fon/Ewe word that described the immensity of the sea.[2] There is even speculation that the name *Imamou* comes from the Mandika and Arabic "Al-Imamu," the Iman who leads the prayers and often the community.[3]

As befits a naval commander, Agwe has many important friends and relatives. Klemezin (St. Clare), the beautiful young girl who brings clear visions, is his younger sister. He is married to two lwa—La Sirene, the lovely mermaid queen of the ocean, and her sister Erzulie Freda, lwa of love and luxury. (Many human women also marry the handsome and gentle sea officer to seek his protection and aid.) Ogou Balindjo—some houses say Ogou Batala—is his loyal second-in-command and watches over his affairs. Some legends say Agwe is the son of President Clermail, a powerful and wealthy river lwa who makes the rivers overflow when he is angry. Although President Clermail was once more widely served, he is less popular today. This does not trouble him, as he has little interest in the affairs of men.

Agwe owns all the lands beneath the waves and everything therein. He and La Sirene reside in an enormous castle made of coral deep beneath the ocean. His sister Klemezin lives in another palace made of mother-of-pearl, while he has constructed still another temple of pink marble for Freda, with lush gardens filled with white doves. All of his homes are beautiful, resplendent with light and ringing with the songs of La Sirene and her fellow mermaids. Those who are taken by La Sirene or her sisters also live here, alongside those who were lost at sea. If they please their captors, they may one day return to the above-water world as powerful magicians, with skills that will make them wealthy, beautiful, and famous.

Working with Agwe

Like Damballah, Agwe is considered a "white lwa." He does not like cigarette smoke and prefers sirop d'orgeat to hard liquor. (Some Vodouisants give him sake, champagne, or sweet liqueurs.) Many houses use images of St. Ulrich, a bearded bishop holding a fish. Others use St. Ambrose or Archangel Raphael. Agwe's colors are white, along with pale sea blue and sea green. Along with his boat, one often finds his conch shell.

At one time most sociétés held an annual three-day beach fet for Agwe in December. A *barque* (raft) would be loaded with cakes, a sheep whose wool had been dyed blue, and other offerings; it was then set afloat to the accompaniment of drumbeats and singing, all accompanied by the blowing of a conch shell. When Agwe comes, he will often dive into the ocean and return holding a fish in his hand—or his mouth! This ceremony is very elaborate and quite expensive, so it is not often held today. Perhaps in the future, when poverty and desperation have abated somewhat, Agwe will once again receive regular service on Haiti's shores.

When Agwe comes, his horse is seated in a chair and given a long oar (or, if no oar is available, a cane or staff). With this Agwe pushes himself along as if he were rowing a boat. Meanwhile, the congregation makes sure to keep the horse wet: should things get too dry, Agwe will depart. While he is a forgiving lwa, he is also particular about his service. Our house once attempted to hold a *maryaj Agwe* (spiritual marriage to Agwe) on the beach in Coney Island. This beach has long been used for religious services: New York's Caribbean community is among the largest in the United States. Drummers had been hired and a ritual prepared—but Agwe was unimpressed with the dirty water and refused to arrive, forcing us to reschedule the ceremony.

To honor Agwe, you can use a boat: depending on how much space you have, this can be anything from a tiny toy ship to an enormous mantelpiece model. Mark *Imamou* on the boat to show it is Agwe's.

You can suspend it from your ceiling or leave it on a table designated for Agwe, atop a clean cloth in the appropriate color. Any naval item—sextants, telescopes, compasses, fishing nets, or the like—can also be placed on an Agwe altar. Whatever you place there should be the best you can find and afford, since Agwe prefers quality to quantity. Mambo Zetwal Kleye (Kathy Latzoni), who is particularly dedicated to Agwe, notes, "He would rather wait for things to be done right than have a sloppy ceremony held in his honor."[4]

Do *not* place pirate paraphernalia on or near Agwe's altar. Agwe is a naval officer and wishes to maintain law and order on and in the high seas. To him pirates aren't charming, raffish rebels, they are murderous criminals deserving death. Also avoid singing some of the more vulgar "sea shanties" around him. Agwe is an admiral, not a common sailor. (We have found that he likes sea-themed classical music such as Debussy's *La Mer* and Britten's *Four Sea Interludes*.) Agwe is a very formal lwa. While Vodouisants call Danto "Mama," Ogou "Papa," and Zaka "Kouzenn," Agwe is always "Met" (Master), even to his wives and servitors.

Agwe must be approached not only with reverence but with respect. This may be discomforting for those who bristle at authority. He is compassionate and understanding, but he demands that we recognize his status and treat him accordingly. Agwe is not our servant or even our best buddy; he is lord of the ocean and we are his subjects come before him to seek his counsel and blessing. If you want to honor Agwe, honor him as you would honor an important and beloved monarch. He does not demand we grovel before him—that's for tyrants, not for true kings—but he expects to be treated appropriately. This has nothing to do with elaborate rules of etiquette; it has everything to do with your attitude and deportment.

Learning how to behave with respect and dignity when in the presence of important people will not only serve you well in working with Agwe, it will prove very useful in the business world. Good bearing and a respectful demeanor will make you stand out in an office full of rude and unhelpful people. If your superiors don't deserve your respect and polite cooperation, you should start looking for another job. Agwe knows that even the finest ship will not go far without a worthy captain.

Conch Horn for Agwe

Je veux désormais vous chanter:
revolutions, fusillades, tueries
Bruit des coco-macaque sur des épaules noires
Mugissements du lambi, lubricité mystique de vaudou

[Now I want to sing for you
revolutions, executions, killings
The sound of the coco-macaque stick on Black shoulders
The moaning of conch shells, lascivious mystery of Vodou]
HAITIAN POET PHILLIPPE THOBY-MARCELIN, FROM
"*SAINEMENT*" ("HEALTHY"), 1926[5]

Before Columbus came to America, the Arawak and Taino people of Ayiti used the shells of *Strombus gigas* (Queen conch) as tools, jewelry, and currency. They also drilled holes in the largest and most perfect shells and turned them into horns. In this they were following a tradition that has been found around the world. In battle Vishnu's conch trumpet Panchajanya brings terror to his foes; blown in peace, it echoes the great "Om" that created the universe. In Greece and Rome, Triton calmed or stirred the waves with his horn; the sound of the conch horn marked the arrival of Hawaiian royalty.

Haiti's 1791 Revolution began with the call of the *lambi* (conch horn). It rang out through the verdant forests as the guerrillas descended from the mountains to the French plantations; it announced rebellions and escapes and warned of French troop movements. As a result Haitians have long seen the conch horn as a symbol of the revolution and of independence. Like Agwe, the conch horn's call resonates throughout Haiti and around the world. A conch horn dedicated to Agwe will be a wonderful gift for him—and a powerful magical tool for you.

To start you will need a large conch shell that is at least seven inches (eighteen centimeters) in length—the longer the better. You will also need a hacksaw, a nail or drill, and some coarse sandpaper; as well as a white cloth, a white candle, and a clear crystal bowl filled with seawater (if you do not live near the ocean, use salt water made with sea salt). Sprinkle a few drops of the sea or salt water on the floor and ask Legba to open the way for Agwe so he can come. Now wipe the shell down with rose water or perfume, then with the salt water. As you do, imagine Agwe's energy cleaning the shell. He is causing it to undergo a sea change and preparing it for the next stage of the operation.

Saw off about one-eighth inch to one-half inch of the pointed end of the conch shell: you want to create a hole in the top that is approximately the size of a U.S. dime (0.7 inches, or 1.8 centimeters). Err on the side of caution: you can always cut again should the hole be too small. This sawing is going to be harder than you might think. Conchs build their shell out of a tough brick-and-mortar matrix of proteins and calcium carbonate that ceramics scientists are still trying to duplicate.[6] When you finish sawing, you will see a structure blocking the hole you have made. Clear some of this out with your drill or nail: you want to allow some air to pass through while still retaining some air restriction. Smooth the mouthpiece with sandpaper and you are finished.

After you offer this to Agwe, you can wrap it in a white, pale green, or pale blue silken cloth and store it until it is needed. Alternately, you can put it on your shrine to Agwe: if you do that, make sure the shell and the shrine are kept neat and regularly dusted. His conch shell can become one of the centerpieces of Agwe's altar and of the room.

To blow this horn, place your lips tightly together, place the shell's mouthpiece to them, and breathe out. With patience and practice you will learn to produce a clear, ringing tone from the conch shell. You can use this to call Agwe when you wish to honor him; you can also use it to banish unwanted entities and "bad energy." Evil things run in terror when they hear Agwe's horn: they know that though he is slow to anger, his wrath is as terrifying and implacable as the tsunami.

If you are not good with tools, you can still get a horn for Agwe; conch shell horns are available online. If you have a little extra money, you may even want to purchase one of the beautiful *Dung-Dkar* used in Tibetan Buddhist ceremonies. Covered with silver filigree, decorated with semi-precious stones, and fitted with a mouthpiece, these conch shell horns are breathtakingly lovely and may be a bit easier to play. And if after all your efforts you can't get a sound out of your conch shell, don't despair! The simple presence of this offering will help to ensure Agwe's favor and protection.

Soothing Troubled Waters with Agwe

Conflicts at the office can wreak havoc with more than your career. Being trapped in an office with someone(s) you dislike can turn your shift into a nightmare. Resentments can simmer and fester for years and decades, spilling over into your personal life and threatening your health and happiness. Leaving your job might not be a viable option, and while fantasies of "going postal" may provide momentary satisfaction, you really don't want to follow through on them.

Situations that threaten your job don't just cause you irritation, they endanger your ability to provide for yourself and your dependents. They bring out a deep, primal fear and an equally deep anger. When you're faced with annoying colleagues, you may be tempted to respond with aggressive magic—in other words, to curse the bastards. But though there are times when you may feel justified in calling out the attack dogs, this typically causes more problems than it solves. The energy used for cursing and aggressive wanga can be hot and stimulating—in other words, it can make frayed tempers even worse.

If your workplace feels like a war zone, you can call on Agwe to calm things down. As a commodore, Agwe is well acquainted with negotiations and armistices. As a ship's captain, he knows what it's like to spend long periods in close quarters with unpleasant people. With his help and guidance, you can defuse open hostilities and make your office a more peaceful place.

To begin this working, you will need a large ceramic bowl. Ideally this bowl will be white, but a very pale blue or pale sea green bowl will also work. You will also need nine floating tealight candles, extra virgin olive oil, spring water, a pinch of sea salt, and some nice perfume. Lotion Pompeii is traditionally given to Agwe if you can find it. If not you can use rose water or any nice French perfume.

Draw Agwe's vévé on a piece of white paper. Do the best you can, but it doesn't have to be perfect. As you draw it, thank Agwe for taking the time to help you. (Remember that he is a very important lwa and has many other commitments.) When you are finished, put the bowl on top of your drawing. Fill it about one-half to two-thirds full of spring water, leaving space at the top. Add the salt, then sprinkle a few drops of the perfume in the water. Float the tea lights on the water but do not light them yet.

Call on Agwe; as you do, light each candle. Feel Agwe's deep, solemn presence filling the bowl and expanding out until it surrounds and embraces you. Explain to him the problems you are having at work. Be fair and honest; while listing the wrongs done to you, be sure to include anything you might have done to exacerbate the situation. Tell him you want all the fighting and conflict to cease. Now pour some olive oil on the water. As you are pouring, imagine Agwe's peace coming over you and those around you. The oil will snuff out the tealights; as it does, feel Agwe defusing arguments and cooling hot heads.

When the lights are out, sit for a while and enjoy the stillness and calm. A few minutes may be all you need or you may wish to spend more time in Agwe's presence. When you feel it is time to go, thank Agwe again for coming and wish him a good journey back to Gineh. Take the vévé that you drew and put it in your workplace if you can. If not, carry it with you in your wallet or purse. This will help to bring Agwe's peace to your job and to your coworkers.

Keep in mind that diplomacy involves compromises. This spell will not magically fix all the problems that may exist between you and your colleagues. Rather, it is intended to provide a bit of "breathing room" and to soothe immediate troubles. Once that is achieved, it is up to you to work to strengthen your business relationships and avoid future troubles. You don't have to be on affectionate or even friendly terms with your coworkers: what is important is that you, and they, are able to behave professionally.

Agwe Pwen for Financial Success

This is an expanded version of a wanga that originally appeared in *The Haitian Vodou Handbook*. It is a bit more time-consuming and labor-intensive than the original example—but when working with Agwe, extra efforts mean extra reward.

Get a white, pale blue, or pale green seven-day (glass-enclosed) candle. You will also need a small clear or white fireproof baking dish and some white sand. If you can, get some Lotion Pompeii, which is the perfume typically given to Agwe. If not, you can substitute rose water or something else that is light and floral. Use this to cleanse the candle until it is thoroughly clean of dust and dirt; Agwe is a very fastidious spirit.

Draw Agwe's vévé on a sheet of unlined white paper using green ink. Green is one of Agwe's colors and will also serve to draw in prosperity. You can glue the paper to the candle or place it on the bottom of the fireproof dish as the spirit moves you. Feel free to decorate the glass surrounding the candle with glitter, sequins, or other items that strike your fancy. You can also leave the candle, which acts as an unadorned lighthouse by which Agwe can find his way to you.

Place the candle in the center of the dish and surround it with white sand. Place all of this atop a clean white headscarf: Haitians and Haitian-Americans typically use the polyester headscarves known as *mouchoirs* (French) or *moushwa* (Kreyol); you can use silk, cotton, or linen if you wish. A square yard (meter) of fabric will be sufficient; more will prove unwieldy later.

Get a white cup and fill it with salt water. If you live near the ocean, seawater is ideal; otherwise a pinch of sea salt in some spring water will be sufficient. Sprinkle a few drops of the salt water on the ground and ask Papa Legba to open the way and guide the *Imamou* to your place.

Now light the candle and welcome Met Agwe. Feel the commander of all navies and keeper of all the sea's riches coming to greet you. His pale green eyes are calm and deep as a placid sea. His bearing is kingly and he moves with the sinuous elegance of the ocean waves. As he arrives everything becomes serene but strange, as if you were seeing it beneath deep water. You are now in the presence of Agwe Taroyo, Agwe the King.

Now that Agwe is present, pour your heart out to him. Tell him all your dreams; let him know the good things you would do if only you had more money. Feel free to share your financial difficulties with him and ask him for help, but be honest. Agwe is one of the oldest lwa, and it is very difficult to pull the wool over his eyes. If your misbehavior or mistakes have led you into your current crunch, be ready to explain why you aren't going to get into a similar situation next time. But whereas Ogou can be gruff and harsh, Agwe is always calm and understanding. If you are in trouble through no fault of your own, Agwe will come to your aid. If you have learned from your mistakes, Agwe is happy to give you another chance.

After you have finished talking to Agwe, leave the candle burning. If that is not possible, snuff out the candle with your fingers when you leave the house. Light it every day and talk to Agwe; let him know how you are doing and how things are going for you. You will find Agwe to be a compassionate and patient listener. You may also find many of the problems that have been plaguing you will be washed away with new opportunities coming in on the tide.

After the candle has burned out, wash the chimney thoroughly with Pompeii Lotion or rose water, then again with salt water. Take the sand from the base. Mix it with some sea salt, some tiny shells, and some blue or green sea glass. If you like you can include other appropriate treasures—one or more loose sea pearls, some aquamarine stones, or anything else that reminds you of Met Agwe and his wealthy underwater kingdom.

Place a piece of fan coral in the candle chimney so that it is sticking out. As you do, feel Agwe's presence gently caressing your new *pwen* like waves lapping against the shore. Feel him filling the sand like seawater moistening the beach as the tide comes in. Then wrap the chimney in the white cloth. In doing so, you are saving a part of Agwe's essence, much as you might take a cup of water from the ocean. You are not "capturing" Agwe (you might just as well try to capture the Atlantic Ocean!). Rather, you are giving him a place that partakes both of his home and yours, a focal point (hence "pwen," Kreyol for the French "point") by which he can more easily come into your life and bless you.

Tie the pwen shut using a couple yards of pale green ribbon (pale green lace trim or pretty braided silk cord will work as well). As you are doing this, feel the essence of Agwe becoming fixed into the object and making it a living being, a spirit that is part of Agwe but which is also an independent entity. Agwe is ensouling this object, breathing his life into it.

Affix the pwen to the cloth with white stickpins, and wrap until nothing is visible but the fan coral. Place this in an area where it won't be disturbed, in a room that is kept tidy. If you already have an altar or shrine to Agwe, this will be an ideal place to keep it. If you don't have a lot of privacy you can put it in a nice box and store it away, preferably after wrapping it in silk and sprinkling some perfume on it. When you want to talk to Agwe, light a candle and talk to this pwen. You will find your communications clearer, and may find your financial position improves in ways you never dreamed possible.

10
Philomena
The Virgin Martyr

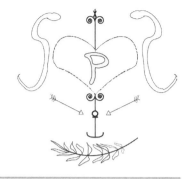

Patron Saint of Education, Social Skills, and Better Business

MOST OF THE LWA can trace their origins to Africa or to the Haitian Revolution. St. Philomena, known affectionately to Haitians as "Manze Filomez" or "Mademoiselle Philomena," comes from Rome. As with many of the lwa, her origins are shrouded in mystery but her power is undeniable. Although she is no longer listed on the Roman Catholic liturgical calendar, she is still recognized by devotees throughout Haiti and around the world as "Philomena, Wonder-Worker" and "Philomena, Powerful with God."

On May 25, 1802, excavators in a Roman catacomb discovered a tomb that was sealed with three terra-cotta slabs, upon which were inscribed the words "LUMENA, PAXTE, CUMFI" and the symbols of a lily, palm frond, arrows, a scourge, an anchor, and a lance. If the last tile were placed first and the words separated differently, the result is *Pax tecum Filumena,* or "Peace be with you, Philomena." Upon opening the tomb, the excavators discovered the bones of a young girl along with a vial containing her dried blood. Since the lily has long been a symbol of virginity in Christianity and the palm a sign of martyrdom, it was assumed that this was the tomb of a virgin martyr. Her relics were ultimately encased in a special statue and brought to a chapel in the small Italian town of Mugnano, near Naples.

There Philomena immediately began working miracles for the sick and the poor. The day the statue arrived, a long drought was broken by a much-needed rainfall. Not long afterward a woman named Pauline Jaricot was cured overnight of a severe heart ailment after asking for Philomena's aid. Pilgrims came from all over Europe to seek blessings at the humble Mugnano shrine, and many found their prayers answered. In 1837 Pope Gregory XVI canonized her as St. Philomena, declaring her "the Patroness of the Living Rosary" and "the Miracle-Worker of the Nineteenth Century." Other popes showed a similar devotion for this newly discovered martyr: Pope Pius IX proclaimed her "Patroness of the Children of Mary," and Pope Pius X (later St. Pius X) gave many costly gifts to her shrine.

Following the papal example, many devout Catholics came to Philomena for intercession and counsel. Among the most famous was Jean Vianney, Curé of Ars, a humble French priest who worked many miracles with Saint Philomena's aid. Vianney frequently had visions of Philomena, built a shrine in her honor, and recommended that others call on Philomena when they had need, saying: "My children, Saint Philomena has great power with God, and she has, moreover, a kind heart; let us pray to her with confidence. Her virginity and generosity in embracing her heroic martyrdom have rendered her so agreeable to God that He will never refuse her anything that she asks for us."[1]

Another devotee of Philomena, a nun named Mother Mary Louisa of Jesus, had a vision wherein she described Philomena's life as a Greek princess brought to Rome. Asked to marry the Emperor Diocletian, she refused and claimed she had already dedicated her life to Christ. Diocletian was outraged and ordered that the young girl be whipped, shot with arrows, pierced with a spear, and thrown into the Tiber River with an anchor around her neck. (Hence the anchor, arrows, lance, and scourge engraved on her tomb.) Yet despite his efforts, Philomena was miraculously spared and many converted by her example. Finally, she was beheaded privately, only to return when the world was most in need of her assistance.

In 1961 the Roman Catholic Church removed St. Philomena from the liturgical calendar, along with many other saints whose historical records were considered dubious. This did not stop devotions to Philomena; her shrine in Mugnano still attracts many visitors, and throughout the world people still call on Philomena's assistance in matters of health, money, love, and other concerns. Cardinals and theologians might doubt the story of Philomena's martyrdom, but Vodouisants agree with Father Louis Petit, who said in 1907:

> How can they not see that the great argument in favor of devotion to Saint Philomena is the Curé of Ars? Through her, in her name, by means of her intercession, he obtained countless graces, continual wonders. His devotion to her was well known by everyone; he recommended her constantly. . . . [I]t is certain, that the soul which animated those sacred remains was a pure and holy soul that the Church has declared to be the soul of a virgin and martyr. That soul was so beloved by God, so pleasing to the Holy Spirit, that she has obtained the most wonderful graces for those who have had recourse to her intercession.[2]

Working with Philomena

Many Vodouisants see Philomena as a little sister to Freda, the beautiful lwa of love, beauty, and luxury. While Freda is very popular (and discussed in greater detail in my books *The Haitian Vodou Handbook* and *Vodou Love Magic*), she is not necessarily the best spirit to call on in money matters. Although she can bring you wealth, it generally will slip right through your fingers—or it gets spent to meet Freda's requests for more offerings. Philomena is less demanding and easier to please. (Of course you should still treat her with the respect due a princess, martyr, and powerful saint!) Money you receive with Philomena's help is more likely to stay with you, especially if you ask for her help in making sure you use it wisely.

In Haiti Philomena is typically served with pastel-colored scarves of light blue, pale green, light yellow, and pink. She also loves flowers: you can give her pink roses, white or light yellow carnations, or any pretty pastel-colored flower. When she comes in possession she dances about the room, turning pirouettes like a ballerina, and will often scatter flower petals on the floor. Her possessions tend to be quick and intense: I have seen her possess five or six people within the space of a few minutes, jumping from one to the other like a teenager trying on new outfits. Catholic churches dedicated to Philomena are often frequented by Vodouisants, since many believe that she is the patron saint of Vodou.

Philomena is particularly connected with the small town of Limonade in northern Haiti, where she first appeared in 1820. King Henri Christophe, an unpopular tyrant, was riding to Mass at St. Anne's Church when he came across a young girl riding a mule. Christophe ordered her to move aside. When one of his aides said, "That's Our Lady," Christophe scornfully replied, "If that's Our Lady, tell her to follow me." Arriving at the church, Christophe looked at the altar and saw three priests who had been executed on his orders saying Mass. Struck with terror, Christophe collapsed with a stroke from which he never recovered. Later that year he shot himself as rebels stormed the doors of the Citadelle, his supposedly impregnable palace. Today a tiny chapel dedicated to Philomena can be found on the site. It attracts pilgrims from throughout Haiti. Wiser than King Christophe, they offer flowers, herbs, and candles to Philomena in exchange for her protection and blessing, then bathe in the ocean so that Philomena will wash away their sins and any evil magic that others may have cast upon them.

Holy cards, lithographs, and statues of Philomena are easy to obtain online or at your local botanica or Catholic supply store. While you should try to find the nicest ones you can, you don't have to spend too extravagantly: Philomena doesn't want you going into debt on her behalf. Give her regular offerings of flowers, candy (she especially likes white chocolate and peppermints), cookies, cakes, and French perfumes—but, again, don't feel that you need to break the bank to keep her happy. Philomena is friend to rich and poor alike, and will gladly accept any gift given to her with kindness and sincerity. She is especially fond of rosaries, and will be very happy if you give her a nice rosary made with light-colored beads or pretty gemstones.

Like Damballah, Philomena does not like the smell of smoke. Nor should she be given wine or other alcoholic beverages, since she isn't old enough to drink and doesn't like the taste anyway. Fruit soda, sirop d'orgeat, or other sweet drinks will be taken gratefully, as will clean clear water. If you have a shrine to Philomena in your house, you should refrain from swearing or using coarse language around it. You also should not have sex in front of her altar; if you live in a single room, you can put up a divider or barrier to protect her privacy and yours. If you wouldn't do or say something in front of a child, don't do or say it near St. Philomena. (In time you may even get into the habit of behaving politely and respectfully when you are away from your shrine: this will make you stand out in a world full of rude and inconsiderate people.)

Studying with Philomena

When St. Jean Vianney first began seminary school, he faced several disadvantages. He was several years older than most of the other students. Because he had grown up in a poor farming community, his education had been sporadic and he had but little training in Latin, arithmetic, and other subjects that his younger classmates had learned from an early age. Although he despaired of ever attaining Holy Orders, with the help of his "dear little Saint Philomena," he was able to pass his exams and become not just a priest but the famous "Curé of Ars," and later, the patron saint of priests.

Today almost all jobs require a high school diploma; many require a college degree or other specialized training. If you don't have the right education, you may find yourself stuck in a dead-end job, unable to get a promotion or find anything better. If you struggled through your school days, you may dread going back to seek higher education. You may be convinced that you will never get that degree or certificate that would make a difference in your life. Unfortunately, you may believe all those teachers who told you that you were stupid and would never amount to anything. You may think you would need a miracle to pass your exams—but with Philomena's help, you may just get the miracle you need!

This spell will require an image of Philomena (a statue would be best, but if you can't get one, a picture will do), and a Philomena holy card. You will also need a light blue or pink seven-day candle, a sweet nonalcoholic drink, and cookies or candy. You can put all of these on a table with Philomena's vévé and a pretty light-colored cloth. In addition, put together some papers on the course you hope to take or the exam you hope to pass, such as a college brochure or your textbook and notes. If you would like, and can afford it, you can also give Philomena flowers or some nice perfume.

Sprinkle a little bit of the drink on the floor and tell Legba that you want him to get St. Philomena to come and help you with your problems. Then light the seven-day candle and say hello to Philomena. Explain to her that you want to do better in school and you would like her help so that you can get an education and make a better life for yourself and your family. Promise her that when you finish with your schoolwork you will give money to the poor so they can go to school too. Give her the offerings you prepared for her. Talk to her for a few minutes. When you are finished, tell her that you have to go and thank her for coming. Now snuff out the candle and put her holy card in your wallet. Take the offerings and put them under a flowering bush or near a church.

Whenever you are studying for a test, light the candle and ask Philomena to help you get a good grade. If you study someplace where you can't light candles, you can just take out her holy card and talk to her. Let her know how important this class is for you, and give her something sweet just to let her know how much you appreciate her help.

She also likes toys, but is happiest when you donate them to an orphanage or children's shelter in her name. Of course you will still have to study, but you will find that you are able to remember things much more clearly and will be able to grasp concepts that may have eluded you before.

Perhaps you don't think you will be able to get the money to go back to school, or don't know how you will find the time to be a student when you have so many other responsibilities. Philomena can help with that as well. Although St. Jean Vianney's parish was poor, his orphanages and charities never lacked for money, thanks to Philomena's intercession. If you ask for Philomena's assistance, she will help you to find the money and time to go back to school and make a better life for yourself. Keep her holy card with you when you are applying for financial aid or trying to arrange your schedule; you'll find that what seemed like insurmountable obstacles can be overcome with a little bit of help from Philomena the Wonder-Worker.

When you have received Philomena's assistance, be sure to pay her back. Give as much money as you can to scholarship funds that will help other students in need to go to school. Philomena likes to invest her effort in good causes that pay dividends: she'll be happy to help you, but even happier if you take her aid and use it to help others.

Getting Along with People with Philomena

As the old saying goes, in business it's not just what you know but who you know. Getting promoted isn't just a matter of having the necessary skill set; it also involves impressing the people you work with. If you don't like the people at your job and they don't like you, you aren't likely to go very far with the company—or even to stay employed with them. (You may think of prickly but talented bosses or coworkers in your workplace as a counter-example. But just imagine how much further they might have gone if they hadn't been so difficult to get along with.)

If you are naturally introverted, or if you've always had problems with social interactions, you may find yourself passed over for promotions that go to your less talented but more gregarious colleagues. You know you can do the job but it seems like no one will give you the chance: your workplace feels like your high school lunchroom, and the popular kids still won't let you sit at their table. Instead of stewing with resentment, or trying to put on a phony chummy attitude that is unlikely to fool anyone, why not ask Philomena for help? She is one of the most well-loved saints. With her help, you'll find that people will like you, too!

For this spell, you need an image of Philomena, a pale pink or blue candle, a nice pastel altar cloth, some candy and cookies, and a sweet drink. Draw Philomena's vévé in green ink on a piece of stationery and place it on the cloth beside a bottle of nice perfume. (Get a small bottle of the nicest scent you can find rather than buying a big bottle of cheap perfume: like her big sister Freda, Philomena prefers quality to quantity.) Do this on a Thursday or a Sunday if you can, but if not any day will do. You should make sure your space is clean before you start this working—after all, you're inviting an important guest to your house.

Sprinkle a drop of perfume on the ground and tell Legba you want to talk to Philomena. Then light the candle and welcome Philomena in. Explain your problem to her. Tell her you want to learn how to be nice so people will like you. Tell her that because she is very nice and everybody likes her, you're sure that she will be able to help you. Give her the offerings you put out for her and tell her that you're going to wear a little bit of her perfume to remind you of her whenever you go to work. Talk to her for a few minutes, then sit back and listen. You may hear messages in your heart from Philomena, or you may just feel her smiling at you and letting you know that she has heard you. When you are finished, snuff out the candle and dispose of her food and drink offerings as you did in the previous spell. Wrap the perfume bottle in the altar cloth and put it someplace where it won't be disturbed.

From now on put a tiny drop of Philomena's perfume over your heart and a tiny drop on your throat before you start your day. The scent will fade away quickly, but Philomena will stay with you. She will help you to be more open and warm with your coworkers and remind you to be nice when you feel grumpy or short-tempered. She will help you figure out when to speak up and when to be quiet and will give you pointers on saying the right thing at the right time. Philomena can see the good in everyone and find a way to reach out to them, and with her help, you will too. Soon the people at your job will wonder what became of that awkward person who used to sit at your cubicle. And the more they like you, the more likely you are to get the raises and promotions you deserve.

If you want Philomena's help, you should also work to be more sociable. Find a volunteer opportunity in your community that requires you to talk to people. Soup kitchens, homeless shelters, boys and girls clubs—they all can use your assistance. This will give you practice in talking to people and will let you help those in need. Once you get into the habit of caring about other people, you will find that people are more likely to care about you. You can learn all the proper words and gestures to make people think you're being nice, but sooner or later they will figure out the difference between real concern and insincere smiles. You don't like it when people are nice to you just so they can get something—and neither does anyone else.

Better Business with Philomena

If you are running your own business, you know how fierce the competition is. According to the Small Business Association of America, only 50 percent of all small businesses started in 1992 were still open in 1996, and only 29 percent were still around in 2002.[3] As the economy worsens, those figures are likely to worsen as well, as business owners who were barely making ends meet find themselves falling further and further behind. In times like these, you can use every possible advantage to improve your chances of survival.

Many Vodouisants see Philomena as a marketplace girl. In Haiti the markets have long been the territory of women. For much of Haiti's history, men who came to town risked being drafted into service as unpaid laborers on public works projects. To avoid this, they sent their wives to town to sell the extra crops and purchase the items their families needed. Women worked in the market stalls, haggling with other women over prices and quantities. Philomena's bright, cheery disposition reminds many Haitians of a charismatic peddler. Thus, her patronage is sought by those who make a living vending their wares. If your business could use a little extra help, you can count on Philomena to assist you too!

This spell should be done on a Thursday or a Sunday, in the place where you do business. If you have a store, do it there; if you work from home, you can do this in your office or the room where you most frequently work. Get a bouquet of flowers for Philomena: pink or white tea roses are particularly nice, but just about any pale-colored flower will do. Put them in the center of a table covered with a nice white cloth, on top of Philomena's vévé. You should also get the prettiest statue or framed picture of Philomena you can find: you are going to be displaying it prominently in your store after this spell is finished. Place your new Philomena image on the table (or near the table if it is too large) with a light blue or pale pink seven-day candle, an offering of candy, and sweet drinks beside it.

Sprinkle a few drops of the sweet drink on the ground and thank Legba for opening the door for Philomena. Then light the candle, welcome Philomena, and present your offerings to her. Tell her that you are glad she came, and explain that you need her help with your business. Promise her that you will be an honest businessperson and always try your best to do what is right for your customers. If you can't make that promise, you will need to seek help from somebody else: Philomena will not help you take unfair advantage of other people or exploit them. If you sell your wares at fair prices and give your buyers what you promise, she will help you succeed even if your competition is not so ethical.

Tear the petals off the flowers you gave Philomena and scatter them around your store. (If you have an online store, scatter them around your computer.) As you do, feel Philomena dancing joyfully about the room and filling it with her energy. You may feel like laughing or dancing along with her—do so but sit down immediately if you feel yourself losing consciousness or dissociating from your body. Possession is an advanced technique and should not be attempted without guidance from a knowledgeable and experienced practitioner—and certainly not when you are alone! Let the energy flow through the store and make the vibration more pleasant and inviting for people who might come in.

When you are finished, snuff out the candle and dispose of the offerings. Place your Philomena image in a place where you can see her as you are working throughout the day. (If that is not possible, keep her in your home and get a holy card to remind you of her at work; but it is best if you can bring the image to your workplace.) Feel her watching over your store and bringing you luck. When you are dealing with customers, ask for Philomena's help in making them feel comfortable so they will want to buy your things. You may find that she inspires you to redecorate your shop so it looks prettier, cleaner, and more appealing. Also ask her to make sure that you are always truthful in your business dealings, and that you always put the customer's needs first. You may feel like that will put you at a disadvantage, but in the end it will work for you rather than against you. People appreciate honesty and sincerity, and would rather work with a business they can trust rather than a cheaper business with a shady reputation.

11
Kouzenn Zaka
The Farmer

Bringer of Solvency

AFTER THE HAITIAN REVOLUTION (1791–1804), the once-wealthy plantations lay in ruins. Leaders Jean-Jacques Dessalines (1804–1806) and Henri Christophe (1807–1820) tried to return the sugarcane industry to its past glory through a system of serfdom called *fermage*. Under fermage, government-owned land was leased to managers and cultivated by workers who were obligated to remain on the land. In exchange for their labor, workers received housing, food, clothing, and basic care. At the end of the harvest they were given 25 percent of the crops' value to divide among themselves.[1]

But the former slaves had little interest in returning to the fields of their bondage. Moving to the inaccessible regions of Haiti's rugged interior, they carved small plots of land out of the dense jungle. Away from Haiti's corrupt, repressive political bureaucracy, they put their experience as field hands and their knowledge of traditional African agriculture to good use. By growing crops and raising animals, they supported themselves and their families through subsistence agriculture. It was hardly an idyllic existence—there was little in the way of education and healthcare, and it meant long hours of backbreaking work—but it was a free one.

Today deforestation and overpopulation have nearly wiped out subsistence farming in Haiti. Poverty has driven many from their ancestral farms into the cities, or across the water as part of the Haitian diaspora. Yet despite this—or perhaps because of it—the farmer lwa Zaka remains a beloved friend, confidant, and protector to millions of Haitians. His peasant roots remind them of the homes they left behind; his strength in the face of unending toil offers them hope in their present lives. To show his intimate connection to their life, he is addressed affectionately as *Kouzenn Zaka,* "Cousin Zaka," or just Kouzenn.

Zaka wears sturdy blue denim clothes, fit for a hard day's work in the fields. To protect against the brutal Haitian sun, he covers his head with a broad-brimmed straw hat. Over his shoulder he carries a straw bag containing his possessions: cassava bread, a pipe, and some tobacco, a scythe for cutting weeds and harvesting herbs, and other things that he keeps secret. Much as Americans might associate overalls with "hillbillies" or "farmboys," Haitians associate Zaka's garb with peasant culture. To show their solidarity with Haiti's poor blacks, Papa Doc Duvalier's militia (called the Tonton makouts) wore blue denim shirts.

Traditionally Zaka drinks *absente,* a concoction of wormwood steeped in kleren (raw rum). Unlike the popular wormwood liqueur absinthe, absente is not a trendy cocktail but a potent medicine. As per its name, wormwood is a powerful tonic and febrifuge, used to kill internal parasites such as tapeworms and roundworms. Zaka Krebs (Zaka the Crab) will fall to the floor and run burning sticks over his feet to ease the pain of *yaws,* a spirochete infection that leads to open sores on the palms and soles of its victims. The peasants living in rural Haiti were all too familiar with these and other tropical diseases. Lacking access to health care, they (and Zaka) relied instead on herbal remedies and folk treatments to alleviate their suffering.

Zaka is not polished or refined; he is illiterate, eats with his hands, and speaks in the slurred, nasal Kreyol of Haiti's most remote areas. But those who take him for a rube will soon learn that Zaka is nobody's fool. He strikes hard but fair bargains and expects them to be upheld. Few short-change Zaka when he has done work for them, and even fewer do it twice. Although he cannot read, he can count—and he's certain to remember exactly how much you owe him and how much interest has accrued since your last payment. When he comes to a fet, he will sometimes take money from his sack and "loan" it to attendees. While this money is believed to bring good luck, it is understood that when he next arrives, he will be paid back—and typically will expect at least ten dollars for every one he gave.

Zaka's roots have become tangled with time. The *djouba* rhythm that marks his presence at fets can be traced to the *Giouba,* a West African dance known in America as "juba dancing," or "hambone." When he arrives in possession, Zaka frequently announces himself with a high-pitched whooping noise that some believe came from the pre-Colombian Arawak people, peaceful farmers who suffered horribly from Carib and later colonial raids. Since Zaka, like "Ogou," is a family name, all these legends could have some basis in truth. Still, regardless of where Zaka came from, he is indisputably and quintessentially Haitian.

Working with Zaka

Two common misconceptions in the West are that Zaka is either a spirit of fertility or a "plant spirit." He is not particularly concerned with ecological or "green" issues; indeed, the "slash and burn" agriculture that characterizes Haitian subsistence farming is largely responsible for Haiti's deforestation and erosion woes. If you offer to raise a houseplant in his honor, he's unlikely to be impressed. He doesn't love plants because they are beautiful or part of the Grand Circle of Life; he loves them because he can eat, sell, or otherwise make use of them.

Zaka is neither the fertile soil nor the abundant crops. Rather, he is the toil that makes farmland out of wilderness, the endless grinding labor of tilling, planting, and harvesting. He does not live in a Garden of Eden or a Land of Milk and Honey, but on a small patch of dirt where a day of bad weather can wipe out a season of work. He is thrifty because he has no choice. When hard times come—and they will come—his savings will mean the difference between survival and starvation.

If you want Zaka to work for you, you will need to pay him and pay him well. Before you ask him to help out, be sure to set out exactly what you want done and what you will offer him in return. Don't be surprised if he wants to bargain with you. Don't agree to anything that you cannot or will not give: Zaka deals very harshly with those who have cheated him. If you cannot reach an agreement that works for both of you, thank him for his time, then respectfully decline his help. It is better to do without than to incur a debt you cannot repay—a rule that Zaka knows well and follows himself.

Like many country folk, Zaka is mistrustful of strangers. He is particularly suspicious of people who are more urbane and sophisticated than he is—and if you are reading this, you are in that group. He always feels as though they are laughing at him behind his back or talking down to him. If he decides you are trying to take advantage of him, he will either stop working for you altogether or give you a painful reminder that he is not as stupid as you thought. A little bit of flattery will go a long way, but don't overdo it: Zaka knows when he is being buttered up and played for a fool. Kind words will only get his attention when combined with tangible offerings.

Once you overcome Zaka's innate mistrust, you'll find that he is a loyal and reliable business partner who will labor tirelessly on your behalf. He will, of course, expect appropriate payment for his work, but if you treat him right, you will find that he returns the favor. Treat your partnership with Zaka like a valuable asset, because it is. The offerings you make to him and the work you do on his behalf are an investment in your future. If you give Zaka the respect you would give to an important client or a superior at your job, you'll reap equally great rewards.

Like Ogou, Zaka is fond of female companionship. Unlike his warrior friend, Zaka is not likely to be swept off his feet by a pretty face. A plain, sturdy woman with a head for business is more desirable, in his eyes, than a beautiful but demanding bride. The former will help him in his fields and in the marketplace; a pretty girl will just fritter away his hard-earned money on jewelry and perfume. You may not think you are attractive because you don't measure up to some Hollywood ideal—but if you are hardworking and thrifty, you may be a beauty in Zaka's eyes. Serving him may lead you to financial success and greater self-esteem.

Zaka can help you to get money when you need it. He can also provide a much-needed voice of reason when you ask for unnecessary items. He does not like credit and has a peasant's fear of going into debt. If you come to Zaka asking him for help in procuring the latest fashionable toy or pretty gewgaw, don't be surprised if he calls you a damn fool for squandering your wealth. When he tells you that, you will do well to listen. In Haiti people call on Zaka not just for work but for his plain-spoken common sense. If you treat him like a worker in your fields, he will do what you pay him to do, but if you treat him like a wise counselor, you will have far more success.

Inviting Zaka into Your House

As the world economy swirls around the toilet, an increasing number of people are having trouble making their mortgage payments. If you want to hold on to your property and avoid foreclosure, you can call on Zaka. If you put him on your land, he will protect your home and your property and bring you good fortune.

However, be advised that if you do this you're going to want to think long and hard about selling your home. When Zaka claims a piece of land, he claims it. To Zaka, ownership of land is all-important. He would rather own a drafty shack and a muddy little patch of ground than live rent-free in someone else's mansion on the hill. And if you give him a piece of your land, he will want it in perpetuity. In tying him to your land, you are tying yourself to the land as well. If you want to move at some point, you will have to convince Zaka that you will be buying better land at your earliest opportunity. (And he still may not want to move despite all your pleading and reasoning: it's difficult for us mobile American types to understand the peasant attachment to the land.)

For this spell, get twenty-one dark blue and/or dark green votive candles. You can find these on eBay or in many discount or craft stores. Put these in a large enamelware basin if you have or can find one. If not, a couple of Teflon cookie sheets will serve the purpose. (As before, make all appropriate fire safety arrangements.) You will also need an image representing Zaka. In our house Zaka is syncretized with St. Isadore, a denim-clad farmer. You may use this or another image that represents a poor, hardworking laborer, along with Zaka's vévé.

Get a pint of white rum; pour some out and replace it with a generous quantity of wormwood. If you grow your own, that's ideal; if not, you should have little problem finding dried wormwood in various herb outlets. Put this bottle beside your Zaka image. Tell him he is welcome to come and have a drink of absente in your house anytime.

Now cook up a big bowl of polenta and kidney beans. If you can, add oxtail and chayote (also known as merlitons). While cooking this, be sure to stir it only with a wooden spoon. You must also avoid eating or even tasting any while you are preparing it. If you eat any, even a spoonful, Zaka will become angry because you are stealing his food; he is fiercely protective of his things. Place the bowl of food beside his absente.

At Société la Belle Venus, we would begin a ceremony like this with three Our Fathers and three Hail Marys, then ask God, Jesus, and all of the angels and saints to watch over us and guide us. You could use similar prayers or, alternately, a few prayers of your choice to the divine as you understand it. What's most important is that you say those prayers. This is a powerful spiritual operation, and purification and preparation are extremely important.

Next sprinkle some water on the ground and ask Papa Legba to open the gate so you can talk with Zaka. Then light all twenty-one candles. Sprinkle your statue with a little bit of water (you can use a sprig of wormwood as an asperger or a dark blue/dark green feather).

Give the image a name—"Little Zaka," perhaps, or "My Good Friend Zaka"—and dedicate it to Zaka.

Next tell Zaka that you want him to stay, that your home is his home and you are going to prepare a place for him. This doesn't have to be a fancy place—he will be quite content with a small table or even a little bit of closet space—but it must be his place, used for no other purpose. Ask him to look after your land and your house—and remind him that it's now his land, too.

You can talk to Zaka any time. He'll especially appreciate it if you pay him a visit on Tuesday nights and tell him what's going on in your life. If his needs are met, he is not a particularly demanding lwa—an occasional bowl of food and some absente will keep him satisfied. In return for your regular attention, you'll find him to be a faithful friend and a tireless worker on your behalf.

Minding Your Own Business with Zaka

In rural Haiti, government officials were threats to be avoided if at all possible. Police officers and soldiers were as quick to rob you as common thieves, and they were better armed. Tax collectors who couldn't get currency would happily put you to work in unpaid labor gangs to work on public projects for the benefit of Haiti's wealthy. Peasants moved to the most remote and inaccessible regions not because they loved the scenery but because it offered them protection from the incessant demands of whoever was in charge that month.

This level of suspicion may seem strange to us. While we mouth the usual fashionable slogans against police brutality and crooked politicians, we're quick to call on law enforcement when we are threatened, and we regularly participate in elections in the belief that our vote matters. That is because these institutions are there to protect us—"us" being middle-class taxpaying citizens. Poor folks, "illegals," and other "criminals" have a much different experience. Police interactions with African Americans tend to be much less civil than those with white

Americans; just ask any black person who has ever been stopped for "driving while black" or being in a white neighborhood after dark.

Haitian criminals regularly call on the services of houngans and mambos for protection. Thieves, assassins, and smugglers will make offerings to avoid arrest—or should that fail, to get the charges against them dismissed or reduced. We may waggle our fingers in self-righteous condemnation, but we should consider their circumstances. A 2006 census by the United Nations Population Fund found that one-third of Haitians were unemployed.[2] In those situations the moral imperative of caring for one's children may well outweigh the demands of a legal system that protects someone else's family. The lwa care little for laws and governments: They serve those who serve them, and will work for sinners and saints alike.

Although you may have a less confrontational relationship with your government, that doesn't necessarily mean you want it poking into your affairs. Nobody wants to be audited by the Internal Revenue Service, even if their taxes are entirely in order. Disputes with your local zoning committee or overzealous town officials can be expensive and time-consuming, with no guarantee that you'll win even if you are in the right. Maybe you can't fight city hall—but with Zaka's help, you can avoid unnecessary confrontations and keep your business safe from prying eyes.

To perform this spell, you will need to have a place set aside for Zaka. You need not share your home with him as in the previous spell: instead of inviting him in to live with you, you are asking him to come in and work for you in exchange for a fair wage. If you have already invited Zaka into your home, you already have a place for him. If not, you will need to set up a small table for him or, at the very least, a box in which he can keep his things and a drawer in which they can be held undisturbed until you call on him. You will also need some absente, Zaka's vévé, a green or blue cloth, and a green or blue seven-day candle.

Place the items on the cloth, and purify your space by whatever means you normally use. Now sprinkle a few drops of absente on the floor and ask Legba to open the gate for Zaka. Light the candle and welcome Zaka. If you are psychically sensitive you will feel his presence; if you are not, you may have to rely on your instincts or assume he is listening. Don't be too concerned: the lwa are generally good about revealing themselves one way or another. If he is willing to work for you he will make himself known.

Now that you have his attention, explain why you have called on him. There's no need to be overly detailed; just describe the authorities you wish to avoid. For example, "I am afraid the tax man is going to come after me; can you keep him away?" Offer him something in exchange for his services. For example, "If the zoning board drops this whole issue, I will buy you a statue and give you half a gallon of absente." After you have finished, go outside and pour out the absente on the ground, then snuff out the candle.

Now that you have Zaka on the job, you have a much better chance of avoiding trouble. Note that this is not a guarantee of success: as every Vodouisant knows, the lwa can only work "as Bondye wills." If you take this as a license to commit any sort of crime with impunity, you are likely to find yourself sorely disappointed and in a great deal of trouble. In magic, as in life, you will find that a little common sense goes a long way. The best way to avoid running afoul of the law is to obey it whenever possible; if that is not possible, discretion and caution are advised.

Saving Money with Zaka

Zaka is a notoriously tight-fisted lwa; when he comes into an unexpected windfall, he's far more likely to bury it on his land than to spend it on some unnecessary item. He is even less likely to go into debt for things he doesn't need—all those savings ensure that he can afford the things he really needs with plenty left over for emergencies. Although he dresses like a peasant and will insist loudly to anyone who will listen that he's just a poor man, Zaka is one of the richest lwa. This spell, from Mambo Zetwal Kleye (Kathy Latzoni), will help you build a cushion of savings that will protect you against hard times.

To begin this spell you will need a bag. Traditionally Zaka carries a makout, the straw gunnysack that is commonly used throughout rural Haiti. If you live near a Haitian market you can probably find one; if not, a sturdy messenger bag will do. You will also need some bread (cassava bread is ideal, otherwise crackers or hard biscuits will do) and *piloncillo* (a block of unrefined brown sugar, available in most botanicas or Latino markets). A corncob pipe and some pipe tobacco are also needed, as well as a few dollars spending money. Wrap the piloncillo and bread in aluminum foil—you are going to leave them in this gunnysack for some time and they may attract mice or other vermin if you don't. Add them, and as many of the other items as you have gathered, to the bag.

Next you will need to dedicate this bag to Zaka. You will need a green or blue candle, Zaka's vévé, and a bottle of absente. If you have any of his other implements you can bring them out as well. Set up a table for him. Sprinkle some absente on the floor and ask Legba to open the door so Zaka can come down. Then light the candle, welcome Zaka, and give him his makout.

When you have done that, ask him if he can watch over your savings for you. Explain that you are going to put your money in his bag so that nothing happens to it. In exchange for his help, promise him that you will regularly put fresh food and tobacco in his bag and provide him with occasional offerings of absente as well. And make sure you live up to your end of the bargain! You may forget your promises, but you can be sure that Zaka won't.

Now get an envelope, a wallet, or something else in which to keep your things separate from Zaka's. Place the first installment of your savings in that bag. Explain to Zaka that you are planning to add a set amount to that envelope every pay period. Ask him not only to guard it but to provide you with his wisdom. If you wish to take that money out for any reason, first ask Zaka if you *really* need it. Explain that this money is to be used only when it is absolutely necessary. (An unexpected medical bill or repairs on the car you need to get to work would qualify, but a sale on those expensive new high heels or that big flat-screen TV would not.) In time this will grow to become a sizable nest egg that will keep you from falling into debt when hard times arise.

Alternately, you can explain to Zaka that you are saving for a particular item. It can be a down payment on a house or a car. It can even be some fancy toy you don't need but have always desired. (But don't be surprised if Zaka calls you a damn fool for wasting money you could be saving for a rainy day. While he will do whatever you pay him to do, you may want to take his advice seriously in such matters.) By putting money aside, you will be able to avoid using credit cards—and running up hefty interest charges. You will also find it much easier to distinguish between things you truly want and impulse purchases.

If you come into an unexpected windfall, be sure to put a bit aside in the bag. (Zaka might recommend you put the whole sum aside.) You may even ask Zaka to help you with extra moneymaking opportunities, with the condition that you will put some aside in your savings and use some to buy him appropriate offerings. Don't expect to win the lottery or find a bag of unmarked one-hundred-dollar bills, but don't be surprised if you get more overtime or an offer for a second job that will help you make ends meet.

12

Ogou
The Warrior

Planning Your Financial Future with Ogou

HAITI'S FIRST RULERS BEGAN their climb to power as revolutionary warlords. After they lost their positions, their subordinates squabbled for control until the strongest took the throne—a drama that has repeated itself with depressing regularity throughout Haitian history. Between 1843 and 1915, fourteen of Haiti's twenty-two rulers were deposed by revolution after incumbencies ranging from three months to twelve years; three others were assassinated. An ambitious officer had many opportunities to rise to power—and to fall spectacularly.

The Haitian army provided career opportunities for black Haitians who lacked the education and social connections required for a job in the Haitian bureaucracy. While the officers of the *Garde* (Haitian Army) were mostly light-skinned mulattos, the overwhelming majority of soldiers were black. Together they became a political force to be reckoned with and created the beginnings of a black middle class in Haiti.

Throughout Haitian history Ogou played an important role. He inspired Jean-Jacques Dessalines to "rip the white out" of the French colony of Saint-Domingue and establish the first black republic; he guided the assassins who killed the Emperor Dessalines in 1806. Ogou's voice has been heard in the roaring of cannons and the sharp harsh crack of gunfire. Revolutionary leader, intercessor, stern taskmaster, machete-waving drunkard—all these faces of Ogou and more can be seen in Haitian culture from the halls of presidential power to fighters protecting their homes in humble village militias.

Ogou was first honored by the Yoruba, a linguistic and cultural group residing in and around modern-day Nigeria. Alternately warring and trading among themselves and with their neighbors, the Yoruba were one of the wealthiest and most powerful peoples in Africa. With the rise of European trade—more specifically the slave trade—their power and wealth increased. The Yoruba Empire of Oyo, which bordered Dahomey, was one of West Africa's most powerful kingdoms: through much of the eighteenth century the Dahomey kings sent them regular tributes of cloth, cowrie shells, and slaves.

But as the nineteenth century dawned, the Oyo Empire fell into decline and civil war. As chieftains squabbled amongst one another, citizens became war booty. The number of Yoruba-speaking slaves on the market increased dramatically. To replace the sugar plantations lost during the Haitian Revolution, new sugarcane industries sprung up in Cuba, Brazil, and elsewhere. Many of the slaves brought to these farms were Yoruba; as a result, the Yoruba traditions and its Orishas (spirits) became the primary focus of Candomblé and other forms of Orixa (religious) service in Brazil and *Las Reglas de Ocha* in Cuba.

Fewer Yorubans landed in Saint-Domingue; thus, their rites and spirits became subsumed as one branch of the *reglaman* (ceremonial order of spirits). Since the French traders referred to the Yoruba as "Nagos," the Ogous are honored as the *Nago nachon,* or "Nago nation"; the spirits therein are saluted as *Olisha Nago,* or "Nago Orishas." While Ogun is just one of the Orishas, in Haiti all the Yoruba spirits are surnamed "Ogou." Some are also honored by Cuban and Brazilian devotees—Ogou Shango (Chango) and Ogou Batala (Obatala), as well as the herbalist and sorcerer Ogou Ossange (Osain). Others come from Haitian history (Ogou Dessalines) and Christian mythology (Ogou Sen Jak, or Ogou St.-Jacques). Still other Ogous are served only by one house or even an individual servitor.

Although each of these Ogous has a distinctive personality and associated legends, like any band of brothers they have many things in common. All are connected with the color red (mixed with different colors depending on the Ogou), fire, iron, and sharp objects. All are known to be fond of women: Ogou Ferraille (Ogou the master of iron, honored in New Orleans folklore as "Iron Joe") is married to the beautiful Freda; Ogou Badagri is wed to the fierce warrior mother Danto.

Those who have studied the Hermetic Qabalah or Hellenic mythology will note many similarities between Ogou and Mars: Ogou represents both the best and the worst of Mars energy. Ogou may be rough, blunt, and sometimes brutal—but he's a trustworthy companion and loyal friend who will reward your favors and attention.

Working with Ogou

The Nago nation occupies the space between the Rada lwa—the cooler, more peaceful spirits such as Freda, Agwe, and Damballah—and the hot, fierce Petwo lwa such as Danto and Simbi Makaya. Ogou's vévé and saint images can be found on peristyles throughout Haiti. Many women pledge themselves to Ogou in a maryaj lwa; in exchange for pledging one night a month or more to Ogou, they gain his patronage and support. The *laplas* (the guardian of the house and second in command) works under Ogou's patronage; the *dwapo* (ceremonial flags) hung in a peristyle almost invariably include one dedicated to Ogou.

An altar to any Ogou will typically include a machete, so he can hack away his servitor's problems and defend against harm. The machete has long been important in Haitian life, both as an agricultural tool and as a weapon. With machetes, subsistence farmers carved plots of land out of thick jungle; with machetes the Haitian revolutionaries confronted plantation owners and later armed French troops. In 1986 a group of Haitian Fundamentalists tried to end pilgrimages to Trou St.-Jacques, a site sacred to Ogou, by filling in his sacred baths with concrete. Their plans were foiled when Ogou possessed several of his followers, then sent the Fundamentalists away at machete-point.[1]

Other items that are often found on an Ogou altar include cigars (smoked by many Ogous, although a few prefer a pipe), rum or *kleren* (fiery raw cane liquor), and an image or statue to represent the spirit. St. Jacques Majeur (St. James the Greater), a mounted knight charging into battle, is a favorite representation of Ogou. Other Ogous are represented by St. George (Ogou Ge Wouj, or Ogou Red-Eyes), Archangel Michael (Ogou Badagri), St. Elias (Ogou Kriminel), or any other figure associated with war. I have heard of Rambo figurines on Haitian Ogou altars; my own shrine to Ogou features a statue of the Chinese war god Guan-Ti.

Many newcomers to Vodou find Ogou intimidating. There are legends about Ogou swimming in rivers of blood; when he is angry he certainly is an implacable, terrifying foe. But when we work with Ogou we need to remember one thing: he's not a killer, he is a soldier. Like any good soldier, Ogou is violent only when he needs to be; he doesn't go half-cocked into battle without a very good reason. He is quite willing to use force, but only as a very last resort and only as much as is absolutely required. Ogou's not going to kill fifty people if he only needs to kill one; he's not going to kill someone if he can accomplish the same task by wounding him; and he's not going to wound someone if he can teach him a lesson by giving him a good scare.

Because we as a culture are largely insulated from violence, many of us have come to fetishize it. We play video games in which our enemies are blown to bloody shreds; we watch movies where people are bent, folded, spindled, and mutilated. It has become entertainment, a way to get an adrenalin rush in a world that is relatively safe and comfortable. But those who see violence on a daily basis know better. They know that explosions involve a lot more than pretty colors on a computer screen; they associate violence not with glamour and fun but with suffering, death, and misery. While they know that sometimes violence is necessary, that doesn't mean they have to like it, or that they won't try every other honorable option to avoid it.

Ogou can teach us about defending ourselves and standing up to our foes, but he can also teach us about turning away from conflict. It's an old cliché, but there really are some things that "aren't worth fighting over." Because Ogou has seen so much bloodshed, he knows that sometimes it's better to defuse a situation than to escalate it. That doesn't mean he's a coward or that he's not ready to do what has to be done. Rather, it means that he saves his can of whoop-ass for those times when he has no other choice. He knows that even the biggest army can get worn down if it becomes embroiled in too many small and petty conflicts. Ogou has been in many tense situations where a hot temper and itchy trigger finger would only have made things worse, and he knows that the most important thing a soldier can have is discipline.

When you call on Ogou, you don't need to worry about him killing or maiming you. (You would have to be uncommonly stupid or uncommonly deserving of a thrashing to get that kind of response!) What you *do* have to worry about is being held accountable for your actions. Like the United States Army, Ogou expects you to "Be all you can be." He will not cut you any slack when you fall short, and when he gives you an order he expects you to follow it. Ogou is not a lwa you approach casually, but he's the most trustworthy and loyal companion you can have. He will look after you and protect you like nobody's business. He will work overtime to see that you have what you need, even if he doesn't give you everything you want on a silver platter. You don't have to approach him in fear and trembling, but you definitely need to take him seriously.

A good place to start with your Ogou altar is a red cloth. You may use one of the vévés or images suggested here or something else that speaks to you of military power and dignity. You may find that you wish to add another color to your shrine. While most Ogous are honored with red and blue, some are honored with red and white, red and khaki, or other combinations. Cigars are generally a good offering, as is rum; most (but not all) Ogous are prodigious drinkers.

Burn a red candle and make your offerings. At Société la Belle Venus, we dedicate Wednesdays to the Nago nation, as do most other Haitian houses of my acquaintance. However, you can talk to Ogou at any time if the need arises: he is a dutiful soldier who is always ready in an emergency. After sprinkling a bit of rum on the floor for Legba so he will open the gate, give your Ogou his rum. Then light the cigar and blow smoke on the vévé; you can also sprinkle rum on it. After you have done this, sit back quietly and *listen*. Let your *konesans* (intuition, inner knowledge) be your guide. If your Ogou asks for a different accent color, a different drink, or a different statue, honor his reasonable request. This is a participatory faith: you know better than anyone else what your spirit wants or needs.

Ogou Wanga for Women

The Ogous are known for their passion—and for the passion they inspire in their female followers. Father Kwellikant, a Breton priest, explained to Donald Cosentino why he locked the Church of St. Jacques on his feast day instead of allowing the pilgrims inside:

> There were constant incidents, perpetual sacrifices. I saw a woman lift up her skirt in front of the saint on his white horse and say "Here I am, St. Jacques! It's all for you!" Another woman offered St. Jacques a piece of soap to wash her crotch (forgive me!). I heard a woman in the dark part of the church say "St. Jacques, you are a big powerful man. The man I live with is too old. His zozo (penis) doesn't work. Help me to find another one." I heard these sorts of things and decided to shut the church during pilgrimage.[2]

Many female Vodouisants marry Ogou in a costly ceremony that requires the services of several initiated clergy members, a team of drummers, and numerous assistants. Expensive jewelry is required, as are elaborate tables and decorations befitting a wedding. A maryaj involves lifelong chastity on particular days (typically the first Wednesday of the month but possibly more) and may require other commitments. Like any other marriage, it is not something to be undertaken lightly.

While you may not be ready for wedding bells, a woman who wants to gain Ogou's special favor can definitely use her feminine wiles to gain his attention. "Sex magic" in the classical Western or neo-Tantric sense of the word—rituals involving masturbation or intercourse with another partner or partners—are not part of any African or African diaspora tradition. However, it is not uncommon for devotees of both sexes to have erotic dreams involving lwa; neither is it uncommon for devotees to seek guidance from the lwa in their dreams.

For this ritual you will need two red cloths, an enamelware or ceramic basin or other fireproof dish that can hold water, the Ogou image of your choosing, and a red candle. (If your Ogou favors a different color for your candle, use that instead.) You will also need a sexy negligee, preferably a bright red one. Get a little bit of rum and, if you can find it, some Florida Water (a spicy citrus-based fragrance). Finally, you will need some clean sheets and a chance to spend a Wednesday night sleeping alone and undisturbed.

First take a shower or bath; when you are finished, make yourself presentable using your favorite makeup and perfume and put on your nightie. Don't feel self-conscious if you don't measure up to some arbitrary standard of acceptable body types: Ogou sees beauty in all women and is sure to find you attractive if you expend a little effort for him. Prepare your sleeping space beforehand by cleaning it and making it presentable. Imagine that you're getting ready for an overnight date with a charming, handsome, and thoroughly desirable fellow—because that's exactly what you are doing! Feel free to make your place sexy according to your feminine tastes.

Place the first red cloth in the center of the room. Place your Ogou image or vévé and the fireproof dish. Place the candle in the dish, then fill it approximately three-quarters full of water to which you have added a bit of rum (no more than a teaspoon or so) and one or two drops of

Florida Water. As you do, smell Ogou's rough, masculine cologne as he comes closer to you. Sprinkle the water on the ground, asking Legba to open the way so that your suitor can come visit you.

Next light the candle; as you do, see the light of the flame reflected in Ogou's polished and razor-sharp machete. You can see his silhouette as he enters: he is tall and sturdy, with thick muscles and broad shoulders; he walks toward you with the tense flowing grace of a caged tiger. You can hear his desire in his quick breaths and feel it in his burning stare. Move the candles and other objects aside, then wrap the red cloth around your head and tie it. As you do, feel Ogou's strong and sinewy arms pulling you close to him.

Next, turn in for the night and go to sleep. Let yourself be lulled into slumber by the candle's flickering flame. Do not masturbate or otherwise touch yourself, no matter how much you may want to. (When Ogou is present, you may find yourself incredibly aroused!) You may have erotic dreams involving Ogou; you may also find that he only wishes to talk, or even that you have no dreams that you can remember. As you do this ritual more often, you will find yourself developing a protective and romantic relationship with this powerful lwa. Record any dreams or waking visions you may have, and be sure to take any messages you receive from Ogou very seriously.

You may be wondering whether a gay man could have a similar relationship with his Ogou. In my experience, every Ogou I have met has been loudly and definitively heterosexual. Other houngans and mambos concur: Houngan Aboudja, a gay man and longtime servant of the lwa, says that while he serves Ogou Feraille and has a deep, caring relationship with him, "He doesn't want to know about or have to deal with my personal life in that area."[3] The Ogous of my acquaintance would not respond favorably to a man who approached them in this manner; they would be uninterested at best and offended at worst.

That being said, there are many Ogous and many sociétés. Some houses believe Ogou Feraille and Ogou St.-Jacques are not brothers but lovers.[4] Vodou is not a monolithic faith; no one can speak *ex cathedra* of what the spirits believe or do not believe. You may do with this spell what you will, and your lwa will respond as they will.

Planning Your Future with General Ogou Badagri

This ritual calls on Ogou Badagri, Ogou in his role as the General. As a Vodou song says, Ogou Badagri "is a political guy (neg politik)" who "shows you his teeth but does not show you his heart." In other words, he smiles or bares his teeth but you never know exactly what he's thinking; he's a strategist and a careful planner. We're going to call on him and ask for his advice—but first a few preparations are in order.

Vévé for Ogou Badagri

Before doing this ritual you should have given at least some thought to your financial future. You should have looked into a few opportunities that seem interesting and at least researched some of your various options. When you meet Ogou Badagri, you are going to give him a report of what you have done to find your way, listing some of the books and other research materials you have used. You are also going to tell him some things you have done to improve your situation.

If you haven't done any of these things (or if you feel like you haven't done enough), now is a good time to start. Ogou Badagri is a skillful leader, but he has little patience for laziness or sloppy preparations. You will need to give him an honest accounting of what you have done. Include some plans for the future and some thoughts on how you might avoid problems that have plagued you in the past. Talk about some things you feel you could accomplish easily, and some things that might be more challenging. Come up with some short-term and some longer-term goals; then devise some possible ways you might achieve them.

Once you have a preliminary report prepared, you can call on Ogou Badagri. Get a red or blue seven-day candle, an image of Archangel Michael, and Ogou Badagri's vévé (see p. 151). You will also need a red cloth, a small red flannel bag, a cigar, and some white rum.

Sprinkle a few drops of rum on the ground. Ask Legba to open the door for Ogou Badagri so that he can come down and speak with you. Next, light the candle and sprinkle rum on the image and vévé. Light the cigar and blow smoke on the image and vévé. (If you can't smoke indoors you can do this outside: Ogou doesn't want you tripping off smoke detectors. If all else fails you can tear up the cigar and sprinkle the tobacco on the vévé.)

As you do, feel Ogou Badagri's hot, harsh, masculine energy filling the images and imbuing them with his power. He sits behind his enormous ebony desk watching you: his expression is impassive, inscrutable, neutral. He may be angry with you or he may be pleased, you have no way of knowing. All you know is that he is listening intently, waiting for what you have to say.

Tell Ogou Badagri that you need his help in achieving your goals and finding a plan. Show him what you have done so far, and ask for his advice on where you should go from here. When you have finished, sit quietly and go over your plans. You may find your attention drawn to things you hadn't noticed before; you may find yourself asking, "How did I ever think *that* would work?" or "Why don't I try this instead?" This is the voice of Badagri offering you counsel. He may be more blunt than you like—Ogou is not known for his subtlety or his politeness— but you will find that his advice is well worth heeding.

Place the holy card in the red flannel bag. Also include a pinch of tobacco from the cigar and a drop of wax from the candle. Now close the bag and put it away in a safe location. When you need to call on Ogou Badagri's counsel again, you can bring out his holy card and light a candle in his name. Don't do this lightly, and don't do this without proper preparation and planning. Ogou Badagri is a general; he doesn't want you wasting his time with things you should have taken care of beforehand.

Calling on Captain Ogou Balindjo

Many people feel a strong connection to Met Agwe and La Sirene, the rulers of the ocean (chapter 9). Devotees make regular offerings to them and provide them with lovely shrines. But despite this they often find that it takes a while for their prayers to be answered. As "white lwa," La Sirene and Agwe are known to be cool, calm, and peaceful—but while this means that they are slower to anger, it can also mean that they are slower to respond to their devotees' petitions.

Vévé for Ogou Balindjo

When dealing with Agwe and La Sirene, you should also give something to their trusty second in command, Ogou Balindjo. Balindjo steers Agwe's ship, the *Imamou,* handles many of Agwe's affairs, and delivers messages to him. Balindjo is also a mighty warrior, sorcerer, and healer in his own right; he is known particularly for his skill with poison and its antidotes. Paying respects to Balindjo can help you to gain a closer relationship with the king of the ocean, and give you a new wise and powerful ally.

To petition Ogou Balindjo, start with a red cloth, a red candle, and a blue candle. You can also offer him a pocket flask filled with a nice white rum and a pipe with some tobacco. (While Feraille, St. Jacques, and other lwa smoke cigars, Balindjo prefers a pipe.) You will also need his vévé and blue ceramic bowl three-quarters filled with salt water (preferably seawater). I've used a Fiesta Ware eighteen-ounce cup for this wanga, but any thick microwave and dishwasher-safe ceramic bowl will work equally well.

Sprinkle a few drops of seawater on the ground, and ask Legba to open the door and allow Ogou Balindjo to come through. Place the bowl atop Balindjo's vévé. Pour some extra virgin olive oil on the water; let it settle and separate out. Now sprinkle the olive oil liberally with Florida Water and ignite it, preferably with a Sabbath Candle. The Florida Water may ignite impressively—be sure to have something on hand to suppress the flames should they get out of control—but they will burn out fairly quickly.

As the Florida Water burns, imagine Ogou Balindjo rising from the sea. He wears the uniform of a naval captain; it is red and blue and decorated with gold and mother-of-pearl buttons. He carries an officer's sword at his side and a sea officer's hat; his face is solemn and care-worn and his green eyes scan the horizon for oncoming danger. He is at the *Imamou*'s helm, steering Agwe's vessel; you can hear the great wheel creaking as he turns it with his strong, calloused hands. He fixes his eyes on you and sets the rudder, then leaves his post and comes to accept your offerings and listen to your petition.

Give him the rum, the pipe, and the tobacco, then sit back and listen to his advice. He may praise you for good decisions you have made; he may call you on the carpet for your mistakes; or he may graciously accept your gift and say nothing at all. Whatever happens, you can be sure that he has noticed your presence and listened to your petitions.

Again, this doesn't guarantee an immediate end to your financial troubles. When Ogou Balindjo grants you a request, he generally expects you to earn it. You may find yourself with new business opportunities, a fat contract that requires a lot of time and work on your part, or the like: you are less likely to get a free lunch. However, Ogou is also faster and hotter than Agwe—and Ogou Balindjo can convey your messages to Agwe and draw his attention to your needs. If you have any messages for Agwe, be sure to share them with Balindjo. When you are finished, let the candle burn out or if that is not practical, snuff it out.

You can take Balindjo's offerings to the beach if you live near the ocean. Alternately, you can place them on his altar atop a red cloth. Keep him near Agwe and La Sirene: whenever you want to talk to them, be sure to offer a glass of rum or at least a candle to Balindjo as thanks for conveying your message. Make sure his flask is filled and blow some smoke from his pipe on his table to heat him up and catch his attention.

13

Danto

The Single Mother

Bringer of Self-Reliance

AGWE HAS ALL THE ocean's treasures and Legba the key to all locks: Danto has little save the clothes on her back and the child in her arms. She isn't as glamorous as her sister and mortal enemy Freda. Her hands are calloused with labor, her face is scarred, and her only speech is a stuttering "Ke-ke-ke" that must serve for exclamations of joy and cries of tooth-grinding rage.

You might think this poor peasant mother had little to offer someone in need of money. And if you were looking for a handout or a free ride, you'd be right. Danto isn't one to spoil her children with unnecessary gifts or to protect them from their own foolishness. But those who need help—particularly those who support children or other dependents—will find Danto quick to anger but equally quick to defend those she loves.

From her first recorded appearance—at the 1791 Bwa Kaiman ritual that sparked the Haitian Revolution—Danto has been on the side of the dispossessed. Scholars claim the slashes on Danto's face echo scarifications found throughout central and southern Africa. Some Vodouisants say she got her wounds during the long war for Haitian Independence. Others say she got them during a fight with Freda: the two sisters have been engaged in a long war that reflects Haiti's conflict between its dark-skinned poor majority and the wealthy, light-skinned property owners.

Danto is the queen of the Petwo nation. Unlike the calm, more peaceful Rada lwa such as Damballah and Legba, the Petwo lwa are generally more fierce, quick-acting, and short-tempered. Some outsiders have tried to define the difference between the two groups in terms of "good" and "evil," but the Haitian distinction of "hot" and "cool" is more useful. The Petwo spirits are hot, fiery, and fierce—and, like fire, they can burn you if you are not careful. The rhythms used to call the Petwo spirits are quick, syncopated, and punctuated with whip-cracks and whistles. Whereas the Rada drumbeats evoke ancestral Dahomey, the Petwo rhythms evoke the harsh conditions of the Saint-Domingue plantations.

In Haiti many men marry Danto; by putting aside certain nights to sleep alone and wait for her visit in dreams, they gain her protection against enemies. She is also believed to have a special affection for lesbians: despite her many husbands, many Vodouisants say that she prefers women. This is not uncommon in Haiti, where it is important to have children. Many gay men and lesbians will marry and raise a family while carrying on same-sex relationships. This may attract the attention of some gossip, but for the most part the neighbors will shrug and say, "It's their life." Haitians are by and large tolerant of homosexuality—and those who aren't are rarely foolish enough to question Danto's life choices!

Danto's husbands and lovers are not as important to her as is her baby daughter. Vodouisants know her child as "Anaïs"; those who are initiated know her by another, secret name. Like many Haitian women, Danto is raising her child alone. Work is hard to come by in Haiti: many men must leave their villages to seek jobs in the city, or travel to the United States, Cuba, or the Dominican Republic in search of work. Their families are left behind to support themselves as best they can and hope their partners/parents will be able to send money as they can. Danto may share her bed with lovers and welcome whatever support they can provide, but she knows she can rely only on what she can earn through her own hard work.

Danto is represented by images of Our Lady of Czestochowa, a Polish icon that features a dark-skinned and scarred Madonna holding an infant. The scars came from a foreign marauder who slashed the icon while roughly removing the gems with a sword. According to legend the vandal fell screaming in agony after cutting the picture, and was still screaming hours later when he died. The "Mater Salvatoris" lithograph, another rendition of the Czestochowa icon, shows a scarred black woman wearing a plain red and blue cloak. Danto's colors are red and blue; she is generally envisioned wearing the simple blue denim dress of a Haitian peasant woman, and those whom she possesses are often garbed in blue denim.

Her vévé features a heart pierced with a knife; when she comes in possession she is given a small but sharp kitchen knife. With this she will gesture to those she wishes to communicate with; although she cannot speak, it is not difficult to read her gestures and her demeanor. Danto is not a subtle lwa; she is quick to let you know her needs. You may find her intimidating at first, but once you get to know her you will soon understand why she is so deeply loved by Haitians, who call her simply "Mama Danto."

Working with Danto

Danto's favorite meal is griot—pork cubes marinated in bitter orange juice with hot peppers and onions, then deep-fried—with a side of fried plantains. Other foods that you can offer her include black beans, *riz djon-djon* (a Haitian dish made with rice and mushrooms), pepper jelly, pan-fried corn and peppers, or just about any hearty and spicy food. Danto is not a fussy eater; she cannot afford to be. Depending on whom you ask, Danto drinks rum or red wine. I have seen people serve her Manischewitz Passover wine or bottles of malt liqueur. Again, she is not particular and is likely to drink whatever is offered.

Her favorite perfume is Florida Water. In Vodou and many other Caribbean traditions, Florida Water is used for banishing and cleansing. Its clean, sharp scent stimulates and focuses the mind, driving away negativity and allowing the participants to concentrate on the operation. (If you want to drive away "bad vibes" from a space, try sprinkling a little Florida Water; you will be surprised at how fast it can lighten the energy.) If you cannot find a Mater Salvatoris or Czestochowa image, you can use any Madonna and child, or any image of a black woman and child that you feel represents Danto to you. Her altar can be covered with a red or blue denim, or red or blue gingham cloth; it need not be fancy but should be kept clean. (Danto is poor, but she is not filthy; like many poor people, she takes great care of her few possessions.)

If you have children, Danto is especially likely to help you. Because she is a single mother herself, she knows what it is like to have a hungry child and an empty cupboard. Danto is also very sympathetic to those who are trying to escape an abusive situation: wife-beaters who incur her wrath may find themselves vomiting blood or suffering some other painful and humiliating fate. She is a fierce spirit but also a maternal one. She does not like bullies and will do whatever she can to protect the weak when they are victimized by the strong.

This does not mean that you should try to use Danto as an attack dog and send her out to avenge those you feel have wronged you. She is certainly capable of doing great harm to your enemies: in Haiti many Vodouisants who "work with the left hand" (do maleficent magic) will call on her services for destructive magic. But are you prepared for the price that you may have to pay for that work? If Danto becomes too hot, she may begin behaving like a *baka* (evil spirit)—if you do not know how to control her or calm her down, she may end up harming you or people close to you. Instead of asking her for vengeance, you will do better asking her for the strength to overcome and triumph. Danto knows what it is like to be beaten and defeated; she knows that sometimes you have to concentrate on what you have left, rather than seeking a vengeance that will hurt you as much as your enemy.

Danto is a loving mother but a stern one. As Mama Lola, a Brooklyn mambo, says, "Ezili Danto—when you got her, she strict with you."[1] She will not take kindly to frivolous requests, nor will she offer you a free ride. Her love is not unconditional; she is not afraid to call you on the carpet if you are being foolish, nor will she hesitate to administer a good spanking if she feels you need it. (And don't bother trying to placate her with excuses: like any mother, she's heard all the reasons why you can't clean your room, take out the garbage, or do whatever else she told you to do.)

When Danto offers you help, she will expect you to carry your share of the load. If you ask her for help finding a job, you had best put some effort into scanning the want ads and putting in applications. She will help you get back child support, but will expect you to take all the necessary mundane steps. She will give you the courage to demand what is rightfully yours—but she will expect you to use that courage and face your fears. Danto comes from a culture where resources are scarce and competition is fierce. She has had to fight tooth and nail for everything she has, and she expects her children to do the same. If you have problems standing up for yourself, you may benefit from her counsel. She will teach you how to assert yourself and won't let you rest until you do.

Danto Spell for Emergency Financial Assistance

We all know the futility of get-rich-quick and make-money-fast schemes—but what do we do when we really need money right away? Medical bills, emergency home repairs, a dying car and a job that's forty miles away—any given day may bring a crisis requiring an immediate application of cash. When you are already struggling, another unexpected bill can become the straw that breaks the camel's back.

Haitian Vodouisants are all too familiar with this state of affairs. In Haiti one heavy rainfall can make the difference between a bumper crop and utter ruin. In times of trouble, they call on Danto's aid. Because Danto is poor herself, she understands their suffering. And because she is a Petwo lwa, she is "hotter"—fiercer and faster to act than the cooler and more slow-moving Rada spirits. This "heat" means that she is quicker to grant petitions, but it also means that she can be easier to offend and harder to control once you get her excited.

Because this ritual heats Danto up, several warnings are in order. As with any of the spells described in this book, you are welcome to add your own personal touches and innovations. However, do not offer Danto your own blood or that of any animal. A bloodthirsty Danto can become uncontrollable and start "eating" people—and she is quick to acquire a taste for the stuff once it is offered. At worst she might start taking it from you, your friends, and your family members. At best she might start demanding regular fets at which she is given a pig—a spectacular but very expensive ceremony. You should also make sure that you genuinely need the money you are asking for, and that you are expending all other reasonable efforts to acquire it.

To perform this ritual, you will need a bottle of Florida Water, a red or red gingham cloth, and a red seven-day candle; you will also need a heavy red wine, a heat-resistant red ceramic soup bowl, and a heat-resistant surface on which to place it. You will need some powdered cinnamon, ginger, cloves, and nutmeg. You will also need a food offering; I recommend red beans and rice with peppers. If you give her griot make sure it is thoroughly cooked so that the juices run clear. Finally, you will need to draw Danto's vévé in red ink on brown grocery bag paper.

Put Danto's vévé down on the table, and put the red cloth on top of it. Put the bowl and heat-resistant surface atop the cloth, along with the candle. Put a small amount of the red wine in the soup bowl, until it just covers the bottom; add an equal amount of Florida Water and a tiny pinch of each of the spices. If you already are serving Danto, you may add any of her other items to the altar as well.

Purify your space and put yourself in the proper frame of mind with prayer and meditation. I would start this operation by saying the Rosary but you may use any devotional method of your choosing. Sprinkle some Florida Water on the ground and ask Legba to open the door for

Danto so she can come through. Then light the candle; as you do, see the flickering light shining off the edges of Danto's knife. Looking up, you see its red gleam reflected in her eyes. Her gaze is firm and unblinking as she waits for you to speak. Tell her what you need and why you need it. Give her any offerings you have prepared for her and thank her for her mercy and help.

Next, light the red wine and Florida Water at the bottom of the soup bowl. (As always, make sure all flammable items are a reasonable distance away.) As you do, feel the heat from the fire filling the room. The glow in Danto's eyes casts her face scars into harsh relief. The hot red wine looks to her like blood; as she smells the Florida Water you see her pupils dilate, like a cat that has just spotted prey. For a long second she stands there, then she comes running at you like an oncoming storm. (You may want to sit down after lighting the wine: Danto may knock you over when she moves forward.) But before she strikes you, she disappears in a fury of wind and fire that burns through every obstacle that holds you back.

Now that you have called on Danto, be sure to carry your end of the burden. Look for opportunities, particularly chances to earn extra work. Be ready to step up to the plate when you are called. If you truly have nowhere else to turn, you can be sure that Danto will look after you and see that you get what you need. This may also cause her to become a regular part of your life, with all that that entails. She may demand that you marry her, or that you become initiated. She may insist that you have a child, or that you take a second job rather than a line of credit. When you ask for Danto's aid, be ready to follow her instructions and realize that she may demand life changes, not just gifts, in exchange for her help.

La Madama

Haitian-American Vodouisants often use "La Madama" statues to represent Danto. These images make many Americans uncomfortable: they hearken back to the bad old days of grinning lawn jockeys and blacka-moor birdbaths. But if you look at these "Mammy" or "Aunt Jemima" statues the way a Vodouisant might look at a religious image, you will find a great deal of wisdom, truth, and magical power.

La Madama wears the dress of a servant. Her hair is covered because she will be sweating from her labors throughout her long day. She is stocky, with shoulders made broad by years of toil, and hips made broad by years of childbearing. Her skin is pitch black—there is no question of her African origins. She may be poor but she is far from humble, and she is ready to stand her ground if threatened. She has seen her employer's children raised amidst plenty while hers have struggled for every scrap. She has no illusions about the world and is ready to fight for what little she has.

La Madama reminds us of the days when racism trapped millions of black people in poverty, the days when skin color could prove an insur-mountable barrier. She forces us to admit those days aren't over: her fierce stare makes us face the role of race and class in our society. La Madama maintains her dignity and her power despite overwhelming obstacles.

If you want to use a La Madama statue for Danto, you should have no problem finding one at your local botanica (or failing that, at your favorite online auction site). You should try to find the Madama wear-ing a red scarf and dress: the Madama in white is most frequently used for ancestor reverence by spiritualists. These statues generally come in several sizes; get the one that best fits your living situation. An enor-mous Madama is a wonderful display, but it can be heavy and hard to keep in a tiny apartment. Better to go with a smaller one if you don't have the space.

To activate your Madama, you can do this ritual on a Tuesday or Saturday. Put down a blue denim or red gingham altar cloth, and place Danto's vévé (drawn in red ink on brown paper) underneath your new statue. You will also need a red or blue seven-day candle and some food and drink for Danto. Finally, you will need a length of blue or red ribbon and a small black baby doll. Purify your space with Florida Water and appropriate prayers to deity. Sprinkle a bit more Florida Water on the ground and ask Legba to open the gate for Danto.

Next, light the candle, feeling Danto's presence around you: She is staring at you through La Madama's eyes. The vévé beneath the statue and the candle beside it provide her with a beacon by which she can find her way to her new home. Tell her she is welcome to stay, eat, and drink.

Next tie the baby doll to the Madama statue using the ribbon. As you do, explain that her child is welcome to stay with you and to share what you have. Talk to her about your home and your family. If you have children, be sure to tell her all about them; Danto loves children. Don't hit her with a list of requests right away—you wouldn't want a stranger inviting you over for dinner and then asking you if they could borrow large sums of money. Take some time to get to know her and Anaïs: spend a few Tuesdays with them and share the details of your life. You'll find that Mama Danto is a good listener and will often volunteer her help without being asked, particularly if you are generous with your time, attention, and offerings.

This Madama statue will become a focal point for your work with Danto. You can use it whenever you need to call on her; it will also become a powerful protector that discourages negative energy and negative people from entering your space. You may well find new opportunities coming your way. You're not likely to come into free money, but you may get more overtime at your job or a promotion to a higher-paying position with more responsibility. When this happens, be sure to reward Danto for her efforts. As you do, you will find that your statue—and your connection to Mama Danto—will become increasingly strong over time.

Danto Money and Healing Bath

I frequently see clients who are suffering from a string of bad luck, money woes, and persistent fatigue, malaise, and low-grade depression that does not respond to therapy or medication. Often they are suffering from a spiritual condition that has begun to affect their mundane lives. Vodouisants are well aware that the two worlds cannot be separated: for us, the divine is immanent at crossroads and churchyard alike.

One healing intervention that I have used is performed "on the point of" (with the assistance of) Ezili Danto. My treatment involves, among other things, baths containing herbs associated with Danto that help to strip away negativity and to "heat up" the client's energy body. This helps improve the person's financial standing and all-around well-being.

The baths I give include Haitian herbs that can be difficult to find and oathbound information given to me by my initiatory parents. However, I have created a simplified bath that can be used by non-initiates. With Danto's help, you can find the strength to overcome obstacles and achieve the success you deserve. This should be done on a Tuesday evening (Danto's night), but can also be done on a Saturday.

For this bath you will need some Florida Water, a little red wine, a red candle, a good quantity of basil, some black peppercorns, some cayenne pepper, and some ginger and cinnamon. (You can use fresh if you have them on hand; otherwise dried herbs from the supermarket will do just fine.) Place the basil leaves in a flameproof dish (Pyrex works well) and set them beside the red candle. Light the candle and ask Ezili Danto to hear your request and accept your offering.

Add a sachet containing the peppercorns, cayenne, ginger, and cinnamon to one cup (250 milliliters) of water to which has been added a quarter-cup (62 milliliters) of red wine and a dash of Florida Water. Put this on high heat and bring it to a raging boil; as it heats talk to Danto, telling her your problems and asking her to bring her energy and endurance into your life. When the water boils remove it from the heat immediately and allow it to cool until it is very warm but not scalding. Discard the sachet and pour the liquid into a dark blue or red container. As you pour, imagine Danto coming into your place and filling it like the water fills the container.

Sprinkle the basil leaves with the warm tea until they are moist to damp but not wet. You will not use all of this tea; in fact, you will probably need no more than a tablespoon (10 milliliters) or two. As you sprinkle this tea, ask Danto to watch over you and protect you from those who might do you harm. Next sprinkle the basil with a dash or two of Florida Water. Feel Danto's power filling the herb and cleansing it of all impurities. You may feel the hair stand up on the back of your neck or notice a sudden flash of energy like lightning striking nearby.

Light the Florida Water. If the basil is sufficiently damp, the Florida Water will burn but the leaves will not catch fire. Imagine all of your troubles and sorrows burning around you, but unable to touch you because you are swathed in Ezili Danto's arms. If the leaves do catch fire, use the rest of the tea to put them out, imagining as you do that Danto is taking care of anything that you can't handle on your own. (Of course, before you start this ritual be aware of any nearby combustible items! Danto will protect you from trouble, but not from your own stupidity.)

After the fire has died out, place these herbs in a hot bath, as hot as you can stand. Soak in that bath, and be sure to submerge your head seven times. As you soak, talk to Danto. Tell her your problems and about all of the things you are doing to make your life better. Ask her for healing, happiness, and success. (If you do not have a bathtub, place the herbs in a bowl of hot water, then stand in the shower and pour the water over your head seven times.) When you are finished, wrap your head in a bright red scarf and go to bed. Do not have sexual intercourse and be sure to write down any dreams you may have.

14

Ghede

Hitting the Jackpot with the Jester

IN VODOU GREAT IMPORT is placed on giving proper honor and respect to the dead. Within a société, deceased members are given rites of passage, then later given homes within the djevo so that they can watch over the peristyle and offer counsel. Service to one's deceased relatives is a major responsibility of every Vodouisant (see chapter 15). But not every Haitian dead person is so fortunate. Many die violently and are dumped in the nearest available ravine. Others die far away from their families and are buried in a potter's field, or are left with no one to pay them proper respects.

Vodouisants believe that some of these forgotten souls are "pulled from the waters of death" and reclaimed as Ghede. (This word can be singular or plural: a Ghede is a member of the Ghede nation, also known as "the Ghede.") These silent, forgotten dead are given a voice; after that, they rarely shut up! Because they are dead, they have no fear of authority nor any respect for propriety and social convention. Ghede is notorious for his foul mouth: his musings on life frequently include many four-letter words and politically incorrect observations.

Haitian society places a premium on polite and restrained behavior. This is not surprising given Haiti's long history of repressive governments: an ill-chosen word or blunt criticism could land you in jail or worse. Ghede plays a role similar to that played by the court jester in medieval Europe. He speaks the truths that everyone knows but no one else dares voice. Because Ghede is outside the established order, he is able to offer unbiased (if not necessarily tasteful) commentary on things. He is the voice not only of the neglected dead but also of the disenfranchised living. When chided for his antics, Ghede will only redouble his efforts to offend: he takes particular pleasure in mocking the pompous and self-righteous for everyone's amusement.

Some scholars have linked Ghede to the *Gedevi*, the original inhabitants of Dahomey. Conquered by the Fon kings, they were consigned to the menial task of burying the dead. Although the Gedevi have long since been assimilated into other cultures in Africa, it is possible that Gedevi slaves brought to Saint-Domingue left their mark on Haitian culture. Still others have pointed to indigenous pre-Columbian Arawak and Taino culture, where the dead were believed to speak obscenely when they talked to the living. (Consider the ribaldry of the *muertos* during Central American festivals for the "Day of the Dead"—a holiday that originated in indigenous culture and, like Fet Ghede, is celebrated from October 31 to November 2.) Given that Ghede are drawn from the ranks of all of the dead, both theories may be correct.

The Ghede are ruled by the Bawon and Brigitte, who are believed to be personifications of death itself (and who are discussed in more detail in my *Haitian Vodou Handbook*). This reign is a rather tenuous one, since the Ghede pay very little attention to authority figures of any stripe. During a fet the other lwa will only arrive at certain times and in response to certain salutes and rhythms. Ghede will show up at any time to steal the spotlight—and anything else that isn't nailed down. He will happily treat himself to Zaka's food, Philomena's flowers, and Ogou's booze, then stumble about the peristyle bumming money and cigarettes from the congregation while singing loudly about how he wants to f--k your mother without a condom.

Ghede's véve features a tomb with a cross atop it. Like many symbols in Vodou, this one has many shades of meaning. It is a straightforward representation of the crosses that are placed above graves in Haiti and other Christian countries. But it also hearkens back to southern Africa, where the cross is a symbol of the cycle of life and a representation of the dividing lines between heaven and earth and between the worlds of the living and the dead. The shovel and coffin are symbols of death, but also Masonic images of rebirth and resurrection (chapter 6).

Ghede's cane is frequently carved so that the top resembles a phallus. When he arrives in possession he will frequently thrust it between his legs and use it to conduct the congregation in songs about the length of his zozo. He also holds his cane when he dances the *banda,* a raucous dance that involves him grinding his crotch in a motion that simulates sexual intercourse. This is more than just juvenile humor: Ghede is a psychopomp who guides souls on both legs of the journey between this world and the next. He is not only a spirit of mortality but also of fertility, who brings not only death but new life. He is interested in erotic humor not only because he enjoys getting a rise out of people, but because that is how babies are made. In Vodou, as with other initiatory orders, the secrets protect themselves. Those who are looking for adult entertainment will find only that; those who seek deeper truths behind the antics will discover those as well.

Working with Ghede

The dead come from all places and all walks of life; accordingly, the Ghede are drawn from different cultures and social strata. In Haiti it is not uncommon to find Spanish-speaking Ghede who come from the neighboring Dominican Republic. While the majority of Ghede are male, Houngan Aboudja, from Texas, has met "Ghede Famn Batis (Ghede Baptist Woman)," an Evangelical Haitian who came back as a foul-mouthed "Church Lady." Among American practitioners I have encountered African American, Italian, and Jewish Ghede; I have also heard of a British practitioner whose Ghede was an English gentleman stationed in various parts of the Empire during Victoria's reign. Because each of us has ancestors and we all die eventually, everyone can work with the Ghede.

Each Ghede will have individual likes and dislikes. They generally prefer their food spicy, since the peppers warm their bones. Haitian Ghede typically eat stewed goat and salted herring with plantains and scotch bonnet peppers, along with cassava bread and *piman,* a drink made by soaking twenty-one scotch bonnet peppers in rum. Your Ghede may favor ancestral foods, or some variant thereof: our Italian Ghede loves hot sausage, while our extremely un-Orthodox Jewish Ghede favors ham and cheese sandwiches, or other equally non-kosher foods, liberally spiced with cayenne. Whatever you give Ghede, make the portions large. There is always room for one more in the grave, and so Ghede always has room for one more platter of food.

Because the world above ground is brighter than the tomb, Ghede often wears sunglasses when he comes. Typically one lens is knocked out, since he walks between two worlds. When asked for more specifics, one Ghede told Maya Deren "It's so I can keep an eye on my food." Another Ghede dropped his pants at a New Orleans party, exposed himself, and said, "How many eyes does this have?" Ghede also likes a hat and battered old clothing in his preferred colors, black and purple. If you give your Ghede these things, do *not* wear them yourself unless you wish to induce a Ghede possession. By putting on his clothing and sunglasses, you are giving him permission to come into your head and borrow your body for a time. This could lead to all sorts of complications for you and everyone around you. (Do you really want to explain to your wife why you were dry-humping her best friend's leg, or tell your boss that it really wasn't you mocking his toupee and penis size at the Halloween party?)

Haitian Vodouisants typically associate Ghede with St. Gerard Majella, whose image features a slender youth holding a cross and staring at a skull on a table. (St. Gerard Majella, who was by all accounts an extremely proper and devout young man, is still trying to live this one down.) You can use other images if you wish; at Société la Belle Venus No. 2, we typically hit our local stores in early November and stock up on cheap skeletons, plastic coffins, skulls wearing top hats, and other

Halloween decorations at bargain prices. I have also heard of people representing Ghede with Mexican *muerto* figurines, images of Grant Morrison's "Jim Crow," Jack Skellington from *The Nightmare Before Christmas,* or even Darth Vader. Since there are many Ghede, there are many ways of representing them; any image that works for you will be fine. If you don't know what to give your Ghede, the best thing to do is ask. Ghede are rarely shy and will happily carry on conversations with just about anyone.

But when dealing with the dead one must show the same caution used when dealing with the living. Not every spirit has your best interest at heart. *Morts* (malevolent dead spirits) may see you as a free meal ticket. They will consume your energy, growing stronger as you grow weaker: ultimately they may make you ill or even kill you. You wouldn't let total strangers move in with you, or lend them the keys to your car if they were living; you should show similar discretion when dealing with unknown dead spirits. Regular banishings and purifications on your work area will help to drive away negative entities. Vodouisants typically use Catholic prayers to do this, but you can cleanse the area using the tools of whatever religious tradition you follow. You should also keep some rue (*Ruta graveolens,* "herb of grace") around your Ghede supplies. Rue has a powerful connection to the mysteries of the dead: it will draw positive spirits like Ghede, while discouraging morts and other entities that would do you harm.

Ghede's Scratch-and-Sniff Spell

I have included very few gambling spells in this book, even though houngans and mambos are regularly called upon to do good luck charms for gamblers. My goal here has been to work long-lasting and pervasive changes in your financial condition. Accordingly, I have treated gambling not as a career choice but as entertainment. Your retirement plan should not involve hitting the jackpot, nor should your children's college fund hinge on a poker game. That being said, there's no harm in having a little fun—a truth that Ghede is only too happy to bring to our attention. Money magic isn't all about grim, joyless work and thrift; every now and then we need to cut loose and have a bit of fun.

The following spell comes from Mambo Zetwal Kleye (Kathy Latzoni), by way of our house Ghede, Harvey. To do this spell, you will need a scratch-off lottery ticket, a black or purple candle, some rue, cayenne pepper, and a drink to make as an offering for your Ghede. (If you want to make some food for him as well, that will be greatly appreciated.) This spell should be done on a Friday, which is Ghede's day.

First, buy a scratch-off lottery ticket. Then if you are female, you will need to wear it in your bra or your panties for a while. (Hence the name of this spell: I have spared you several of Harvey's unprintable comments.) Men who wish to call on Ghede's services can instead sprinkle the ticket with bay rum or cheap aftershave in which you have placed some rue and red pepper. Don't try to "improve the spell" by doing both—you really don't want cayenne on any sensitive body parts.

When you are ready to begin the spell, put the lottery ticket out on the table with Ghede's vévé, the candle, and the offerings you have prepared. Sprinkle a little bit of the drink on the floor and ask Bawon La Croix to send your Ghede up to your house. Although Legba opens the gates for the other lwa, the Bawon is in charge of the Ghedes. Light the candle so Ghede can find his way to your place. When he arrives you'll sense his presence, no matter how un-psychic you may consider yourself. Ghede may be described with many words, but "subtle" is not among them. When he comes he is difficult to ignore—and if you try, he will make it impossible.

Talk to your Ghede for a while, and be sure to ask his name. (Ghede are almost always male, although there are some female Ghede.) Ghede go by many nicknames. Société la Belle Venus's Ghede goes by Brav Ghede; other Ghede names include Ghede Nibo, Ghede Arapice de la Croix, and Ghede Gwo Zozo nan Crek Tone de la Croix (Ghede Big Dick in the Pussy by Thunder of the Cross). Most Ghede have the surname "de la Croix" (of the cross), but I know one Jewish Ghede who goes by the last name "Zetwal" (de l'etoille, or "of the star").

Next, promise your Ghede that you will use 10 percent of the proceeds from your lottery ticket to buy alcohol for him. Then, scratch off your ticket and see what you have won. If you haven't won anything, then your Ghede won't be drinking this week; but if you have, 10 percent goes to buying booze for him. You can repeat this every time you play the lottery. With Ghede's help, you may well find yourself winning more than you ever expected.

Should you have really big winnings, you may want to hold a *mangé pov,* or meal for the poor, in Ghede's honor: give a sizable donation to a local soup kitchen in memory of your Ghede. (And let's hope his name isn't something that will embarrass you and the organizers too unduly.) But if you do make this offering, be sure you also save enough money for plenty of alcohol: if your winnings are high enough, a few cases of rum and a large bag of hot peppers might well be in order.

One final note: there is a big difference between recreational and compulsive gambling. If your gambling is driving you into debt, you don't need this or any other good luck spell. Rather, you need to contact your local chapter of Gamblers Anonymous and take whatever steps are necessary to break your addiction.

Heating Up Your Business with Ghede

Many businesses live and die on excitement. In an overstimulated culture, it's easy to lose the interest of a jaded crowd and become old news. Last year your club was packed; this year the trendsetters are partying at a new establishment, for example. Or your restaurant's business is down 30 percent this year, as your former patrons flock to the new place down the street. Your boutique was the toast of the fashionable set last spring, but today you are barely paying your lease. Instead of giving up hope, why not try bringing back some of that sparkle? With Ghede's help, you can give your tired old business a rebirth and make it a hot place to be.

Get a bottle of white rum and twenty-one Scotch bonnet peppers. These should be available at your local grocery store: they have a squashed bell shape that reminds many of the Scottish "tam o'shanter" hat. You will also need Ghede's vévé (drawn in black ink), a black or purple candle, and a black or purple ribbon—the older and more moth-eaten the better. Finally, you should also wear latex gloves to protect your skin from the fiery concoction you are about to create. Do this spell on a Friday night. If possible do it in your workplace, but if you can't, do it at home and finish it at work.

Pour off a fair bit of the rum into a glass; then sprinkle a few drops on the ground for Bawon La Croix and explain that you need assistance from your Ghede. Next, light the candle and welcome Ghede in. As you do, begin loading the peppers into the rum. (They are likely to crack as you squeeze them into the bottle. That is fine, since it will ensure that more capiscum gets into the mix, thereby producing a hotter batch of piman.) Tie the ribbon around the bottle's neck, as you do feel Ghede's energy pouring into it. As you tighten the knot, you strengthen the connection between Ghede and this bottle, and ensure that he will always be near his favorite beverage.

Pour a second glass of the piman for Ghede. Explain to him that you need his assistance in drawing people to your business so that you can be successful. Now take the bottle and sprinkle piman on your doorstep. As you do, imagine your Ghede standing outside the door like a carnival barker, grinning broadly as he draws people into your establishment. Continue sprinkling the piman around the business. If you work from home, sprinkle a few drops around your office—but be careful, since piman will stain carpets and eat through the varnish on your hardwood floors. When Ghede arrives at a fet, he will frequently swill this stuff like water or wash his face in it like it was aftershave; anyone faking this possession would soon regret their act.

A very little bit will do: you are not trying to make your workplace smell like peppered rum, but to draw down Ghede's energy. A sprinkle will be sufficient to mark the place for Ghede. More than that and you run the risk of stinking up the place and driving away customers instead of attracting them. I have seen an angry Ghede take a mouthful of piman and *fumé* (spray) the congregation, who immediately began choking like they had been hit with tear gas. As with everything else in money magic, moderation is key.

Now that you have a bottle of piman, use it wisely. Make regular offerings to your Ghede and be sure to sprinkle more piman about the place whenever you feel like business may be slowing down. If you would like, you can decorate the bottle and refill it after Ghede drains it—and given his taste for booze, he will drain it sooner than you might think. You can draw his vévé on the bottle with a glass marker, or you can paste an appropriate picture over the label. In Haiti, elaborately decorated *bouteys lwa* (lwa bottles) are frequently used to store libations for the spirits. Yours need not be fancy: Ghede is more concerned with what is inside the bottle than the outside. But in decorating it you increase the power of the bottle as a magical object, and by extension the power of everything that is stored inside it.

Harvey DelCruccio's Spell for Working Girls

While money can't buy you love, it certainly can purchase sexual favors. Technological breakthroughs have provided new opportunities in webcam and phone sex work. Meanwhile more traditional lines of work—escort services, massage parlors, strip clubs, and the like—provide many with a lucrative if not entirely respectable living. But this is hardly easy money. Many sex workers deal with dangerous, abusive clients and supervisors on a daily basis, with little help from indifferent or openly hostile law enforcement officers. They may need a little bit of extra help to ensure their prosperity, safety, and sanity.

The following advice comes from our house Ghede, Harvey DelCruccio (Plate 13). Harvey wishes to share his expertise with any ladies who might find themselves in need of his services. Since he has used your services on more than a few occasions, he thought it only fair that he return the favor:

First of all, don't let nobody make you feel bad about yourself on account of what you do for a living. Any guy what looks down on you is only proving he ain't worthy of your time. A real gentleman understands times is tough and a lady's got to do what she's got to do.

If you need a little help from Ol' Harv, I'll be happy to oblige. Set out a nice plate of grub and a drink: if I can't make it, I'm sure one of my buddies will take you up on your offer. There's plenty of fellas want to help out a lady on both sides of the dirt. Take your favorite necklace or some jewelry you like and leave it on the table alongside our grub. We ain't going to steal it or nothing like that: we're just going to leave a little something extra on it so it will remind you of us whenever you wear it. (And no, before anyone asks, we ain't leaving that on it. That ain't a gentlemanly thing to do.)

Light a candle so we can find our way to your place, then set yourself up a plate and sit down and have a meal with us. Everyone knows the best way to a fella's heart is through his stomach. (Maybe it's the second best way, but who's counting?) Wear something nice because every guy likes it when a lady dresses up for him. When you're done, you can put the food in your yard and put out the candle.

Make sure you wear your jewelry whenever you're on the job: When you got that on, you'll have one of us looking out for your best interests. We can be real good at making your clients open up their wallets and give you what you got coming. Times is tough, and if you got to rely on tips for a living they can be even tougher.

We're especially good at taking care of bums what don't know how to treat a lady right. Some fellas don't know their manners till they get a little education upside their head. And that goes for the boys in blue too. You give some guys a badge, they start thinking they can throw their weight around and be disrespectful of the people what pay their salary and their bribes too. If you got one of us working for you, you ain't quite so likely to run into that sort of trouble and if you do, it ain't so likely to be serious. If Officer Flatfoot can't show up to court on account of injuries or unexpected illness or something, they usually throw the charges out. Ol' Harv knows a thing or two about this, even though he wasn't never in your line of work. (And before anyone gets bent out of shape, I ain't advocating violence against the police in general, just the ones what deserve it, is all.)

You ought to make time for a regular dinner date: we're happy to visit any time there's food on the table and a pretty lady serving it. And if you don't think you're pretty, you just been listening to the wrong fellas is all. Just cause you don't look like you ain't had a decent meal since last year don't mean nothing. Real men like their girls with some curves. I know them fashion designers is always taking pictures of models what look like little boys, but that just goes to prove Ol' Harv's point.

Speaking of which, I know we got some fellas out there working in the industry too. I ain't gonna be able to be of too much assistance to you, but I'm sure you can find a fairy Ghede what will be able to help out. And before anyone asks, I ain't got nothing against youse, it's just that I ain't like that, I'm a normal guy.

15

The Ancestors

Learning from the Hardships of the Past

OUR CULTURE FAVORS PEOPLE who "rise above their beginnings" and reinvent themselves on their way to greatness. The idea that we are defined by our lineage is distasteful. It brings up many of the bugbears that have long haunted our collective psyche; racism, class distinctions, the idea that everyone is not created equal, and that accidents of birth may mean the difference between success and failure. We like to believe that we live in a land of opportunity, where one's parentage counts for less than individual merit, drive, and determination to get ahead. Who you are as a person is what counts: your family background is irrelevant. Vodouisants, by contrast, see individuals not as discrete entities but as part of an ongoing process. We are born to carry on the work of our ancestors and to pass on the torch to the children who will take up our burden when we pass on.

Vodou developed in a culture where family ties were often ripped asunder. The slaves who came to Saint-Domingue were torn from their families and brought to the plantations. There they were thrown among strangers: it was standard practice to gather slaves from different ethnic and linguistic backgrounds to limit the possibility of organized rebellion. Parents could be separated from their children at the master's whim. Legal marriages were out of the question and monogamy was possible only if an overseer did not take an interest in your partner.

Today Haiti's ravaged economy regularly separates families: unable to find employment in their deforested and flooded villages, spouses and children are left behind as their caregivers are forced to relocate in search of work. Yet family ties are still cherished, and service to one's living and dead relatives is an important cornerstone of Vodou culture. In a harsh and impoverished environment, one's survival often depends on family support. Those without family are not "lone wolves" or "rugged individualists"; they are likely to die of starvation or predation.

While our culture is more prosperous, our families are not necessarily more stable. In America, 49 percent of all marriages end in divorce (Canada is doing only slightly better, with a 45 percent divorce rate). The number of American children living with both parents decreased from 85 percent to 68 percent between 1970 and 1996. About half of all children will witness the breakup of their parents' marriage: of these, nearly half will also witness a parent's second divorce.[1] In the nineteenth and early twentieth centuries, it was common to see three generations living under the same roof, with other family members living close by. Today many American families can be spread across several time zones, with Dad and his second wife on the East Coast, Mom and her new husband living in Chicago, Junior in San Francisco, Sis in Phoenix, and the grandparents in Florida adult living communities.

With all this separation, it's easy to feel rootless and disaffected. It's not for nothing that our era has been called the "age of alienation." We live in large houses but never speak to our neighbors. Between commuting and overtime, we may see our children less than we see the security guard who protects our gated community. We work in cubicles with strangers and interact with our relatives through occasional phone calls or e-mails, if we interact with them at all. We seek to distract ourselves from our emptiness with bigger and more expensive luxuries: we hope that toys and indulgences will provide a substitute for quality parenting time.

The solution to this is not an idealized Norman Rockwell view of the family: Vodou is a practical faith, not one built on pleasant fictions. What we need is not a return to a golden age that never was, but a recognition of who we are and where we came from. We do not need to idealize or sugarcoat our ancestors. Rather, we need to pay them proper respect and understand the forces that motivated them and that motivate us. Until we know where we came from, we will never know where we are going or how we should get there.

Our lives have meaning only in the context of those who came before us and those who are to come after us. This does not imply that we are limited to going no further than our family background will allow. Rather, it means that we have a responsibility to take what we have been given and use it to best advantage so that we will leave our progeny in a better place.

Working with the Ancestors

In rural Haitian villages, family graves are typically located within the *lakou* (compound). Small sitting rooms are often built above the tombs of particularly important family members or in the graveyard so those who wish to commune with their ancestors can spend some time above their graves in quiet meditation. But as poverty has forced many Haitians off their land, this connection has become more difficult. It is especially hard for those who are living in the Haitian diaspora as undocumented immigrants. If they return to their ancestral homes, they might not be able to return to their families and jobs in Montréal or Miami.

Vodou is both a syncretic and a practical faith. Unable to make the trek home, many Haitian Vodouisants in the diaspora have begun using the "White Table," or *boveda,* a practice they learned from Cuban *espirit-istos* influenced by the French spiritualist Alain Kardec. The White Table allows them to maintain a concrete link with their forebears even though their graves are an ocean away. It can offer you the same connection to your ancestors, reminding you of your roots and providing a means by which you can communicate with them and seek their assistance.

The White Table Spell

A White Table can be set up on any available table or shelf. Clean the surface using water to which you have added a few drops of Florida Water or lemon juice. If you want to follow the lead of Haitian Vodouisants, also add a few drops of your own urine. While this may seem repulsive or disrespectful, there are good magical reasons behind it. As a bodily fluid, urine establishes a link between you and those who share your ancestry. Unlike offerings of blood, it does not make you vulnerable to any troubled spirits who might wish to feed off you. Urine is also a powerful cleanser used in many traditions around the world.

Now place a clean white cloth on the table, and add any photos of deceased loved ones. Do not put any pictures of living people on your White Table—this shrine is strictly for the dead. Also add things that were important to your ancestors while they were living. A slide-rule for your great-uncle the physicist, a thimble and some sewing supplies for your grandmother who loved making quilts—the possibilities are endless and limited only by your imagination. (Be careful about giving them things that were important to their lives in a positive way. For example, if your great-grandfather was a compulsive gambler, you may not want to give him a deck of cards or a pair of dice. Serve him instead with other things that he enjoyed which were not so destructive for him.)

Add a few glasses of clean water to your table. If you'd like, you can prepare favorite foods for your ancestors but don't add salt. Also place some holy books or symbols representing your ancestral faith—a rosary if your family was Catholic, a *Book of Mormon* if Mormon, and so forth. It doesn't matter whether you are still practicing that faith; you are giving these to your ancestors in honor of their beliefs. Say some prayers to purify your space; use prayers of both your current religious tradition and (if different) the faith of your forefathers.

Once you have your White Table erected, the best way to activate it is through regular usage. Sit down and talk with your ancestors regularly. Talk with your living relatives and get as much information as you can about your family tree. Then talk to your deceased relatives about what you have learned, and see what information they can add. As you share details of their past, be sure to let them know what is going on in your present and what you hope to accomplish in the future. They will appreciate knowing this: since you are of their lineage, they have a vested interest in seeing you succeed, and will do what they can to help you.

The ancestors lived on this material plane; hence they are less remote and easier to reach than spirits who have never incarnated in a human body. This means they can work more quickly for you if they take an interest in your cause. But it also means that they can retain many of their human failings. Crossing over to the other side may give them a different view on the world, but it does not mean they are rid of all of their prejudices or weaknesses. You will have to take this into account when calling on them. They may have difficulties understanding the differences between contemporary society and their time: their advice may sometimes be sincere and well meaning but completely wrong. As with living relatives, you will generally find that the best course of action with your ancestors is an indulgent smile while agreeing to disagree.

Thrifty Living with the Ancestors

You may have enjoyed your grandfather's romantic tales of life during the Great Depression, or you may have been regaled with stories about how kids today don't appreciate what it's like to walk six miles barefoot to school. But did you ever think about putting those lessons into practice—or traveling down your roots to learn from your ancestors? No matter how bad your current financial situation is, you have ancestors who lived through worse. The potato famine, pogroms in Russia and Eastern Europe, life under Jim Crow laws—no race or ethnicity has been spared the burden of history. But despite those difficulties, your ancestors were able to survive and to pass the torch on through the bloodline to you. By tapping into their wisdom, you can acquire skills that will serve you well in your current situation.

Once upon a time almost everyone knew how to darn a sock, fix a split seam, or mend a tear. Clothing purchased in stores was expensive and so most clothes were made at home. Instead of closets filled with unworn clothing, most owned just a few outfits and had to make them last as long as possible. (And they did this with laundry soap and washboards instead of washing machines!) Today we go to big-box stores or the mall and find cheap, readily available clothing manufactured in sweatshops around the world. When something gets torn, we throw it out and purchase a new one. Not only does this perpetuate injustice and oppression in the countries where these disposable clothes are made, it wastes money that we could better spend on other needs. Imagine how much you could save on clothing if you fixed things instead of throwing them out? You might even be able to buy better, longer-lasting outfits and take better care of them.

If you are living the single professional lifestyle, you may be subsisting on a steady diet of take-out food. This is both expensive and unhealthy. You would be much better off cooking your own food and reserving your restaurant visits for special occasions. Maybe you can't cook, and your parents can't cook—but if you go back far enough in your family line, you're bound to find people who were able to feed a large and growing family on a small and often shrinking budget. If your great-grandmother could feed eight children and a hard-working husband over a tenement stove, she can show you how to make an inexpensive but nutritious meal in your tiny studio's kitchen.

You may be generations removed from the family business, remembering only vague tales of how your thrice-removed great-grandparents once owned a hotel that was burned down by Sherman's troops during the Civil War, or stories about how your family had a haberdashery store before they emigrated. By establishing contact with your ancestors, you can tap into their business acumen and apply it to your present situation. You may even find yourself taking up a whole new line of work you never imagined, as you draw from knowledge buried for decades or even centuries.

To do this Thrifty Living with the Ancestors spell, all you need is your White Table and some quiet time for meditation. If you wish to speak to a particular departed loved one, you may call out his or her name; otherwise you can just state that you are here to speak to those who have gone to their rest before you. Bring offerings to your ancestors and talk to them; imagine you are visiting a kindly relative's home, because you are. Let them know why you have come. Explain your problems and ask for their advice. Then, when you are finished talking, sit back and listen.

This can be a challenge for people raised in our overstimulated culture: you may want to fill the interior and exterior silence with something. Resist that impulse, and let yourself be quiet but aware. You may have trouble calming your racing thoughts and impressions, but do not try to do so. Rather, let them rise to the surface of your mind and then pass into nothingness. In time the chatter and static will fade and you will hear the voices of those whose blood runs through your veins. They may speak to you in words, or in the language of the heart: you may receive deep inspirations or hunches about what you should do next.

Combine these inspirations and words with your own research. You may find information about sewing, cooking, and other thrifty household skills in old books, "guides for young ladies," and home economics textbooks, which can be very valuable and bought for very little from used bookstores, thrift shops, garage sales, or online auctions. With a bit of practice—and some help from the spirits who watch over you— you may find that you pick up these old techniques more quickly and thoroughly than you ever thought possible. You may also find that your attitude toward money and your spending habits change for the better as you draw upon the hard-earned wisdom of your forebears.

Healing Family Money Curses

Ancestral veneration does not involve pretending that your family is without faults. Instead, it requires recognizing their shortcomings and working to overcome them. Your ancestors' influence on you is for both good and ill. You have inherited many of their strengths, but you are also carrying some of their weaknesses. If your family had chronic financial problems, you may not have learned the art of saving money or using credit wisely. Replaying what you learned as a child, you find yourself facing the same troubles that plagued your parents and grandparents.

You may have grown up in a family where you got little attention but lots of presents. As a result, you learned to fill your need for love with possessions. Or you may have grown up with parents who had failed in business and allowed that failure to define their being. Growing up surrounded by their bitterness, you may have followed their example. You may have made money the defining factor of your self-esteem: if you are financially successful you feel you are successful in life, and if you are not, you see yourself as inherently bad and worthless. But since there are always people with more money than you, you can never feel truly successful or worthy.

Substance abuse can be passed down family lines. If your family has struggled with addiction issues for generations, you may struggle with them as well. You may feel you have escaped the burden: after growing up with alcoholic parents, you don't drink at all. But addictions can morph and remanifest in new forms. You may not drink compulsively or numb your worries with pills, but do you spend obsessively? You may behave like a "dry drunk"—one who has quit drinking but still maintains the dysfunctional beliefs and behavior patterns that caused the problem in the first place.

If your relationship with your family was rocky, you may be carrying those scars. Those who grew up in emotionally abusive homes may have spent much of their childhood being told they were worthless and would never amount to anything. This may become a self-fulfilling prophecy. If you expect to fail at everything you do, the universe will often oblige you. If you assume your situation is hopeless, you are unlikely to expend the effort to prove yourself wrong. You may also have been raised with constant unrealistic expectations, that no matter what you did, it was never quite good enough. In response, you may still be driving yourself toward a goal you can never reach, or you may have given up altogether and resigned yourself to being a "failure" despite accomplishments that most would consider success.

You may also have fallen into a trap that is common to the children of dysfunctional families. Since you have no experience of how happy families behave, you are forced to seek models elsewhere. Your model may be based on wealth; you may think that you would have the idealized sitcom family if only you had a bigger house in a nicer neighborhood. It may also be based on poverty; since money didn't solve your family's woes, perhaps a lack of money would cure the problems. You may feel guilty about your prosperity: that your success would only serve to highlight your parents' failure. Or you may see money as a way of getting back at them: if you have enough money, you will prove to them once and for all that you actually were worth something all along.

To address these problems, sit down at your White Table (or by a family grave, if you live near one or happen to be in the vicinity). Explain to your ancestors how these problems are affecting you, and ask for their assistance in learning new and more effective ways to deal with these issues. When you have done that, be sure to fulfill your end of the deal. Do whatever work is necessary to learn how to handle money more wisely. That may involve counseling or joining a support group; it will certainly require struggle and discipline on your part. When we work with the ancestors, we engage in a process of co-creation: their help and guidance are combined with our efforts to fulfill our joint destiny.

You should also know that you are under no obligation to place any specific ancestor on your White Table. You need not give honor to relatives who abused you, nor do you need to forgive unforgivable behavior. Concentrate instead on those who made a positive difference in your life, giving them the attention and respect they deserve. Your time and efforts are valuable, and so are you. You need not squander yourself on those who do not deserve you. Learning this lesson will be the first step in healing many of those wounds.

Genealogy and Graveyards

A White Table is a wonderful tool for communing with your ancestors—but if you live near a cemetery where family members are interred, you should also pay regular visits to their graves. Keep the gravesites clean and weeded; make sure that they are decorated regularly and are honored with the appropriate religious ceremonies—memorial Masses if they are Catholic, Yahrzeit candles if they are Jewish, and so on. You should also take a tiny bit of dirt from their graves and place it on your White Table (you can put it in a perfume vial or a small box). This will provide an even more direct link to your ancestors: in African traditions, dirt, particularly graveyard dirt, is believed to carry a powerful magical charge.

Try to trace your ancestry back as far as you can. Numerous genealogy sites can help you discover relatives you never knew about. Try to learn more than just names and dates (although those are important). Try to study the history that swirled around them and how they coped or failed to cope with those events. Did your great-grandparents come out to California in search of gold, or were they loyalists who ran for their lives to Ontario? In what wars did your ancestors fight, and on what side? By learning which forces shaped their lives, you can gain insight into the forces that shape yours.

If you do not live near your ancestral graves, you should consider making a trip to see them. Haitian Vodouisants who are able to do so make frequent voyages back to their family homes. This may be as simple as a trip to the neighboring state in which your grandparents were buried, or as elaborate as a six-week journey to various European churchyards. Gather dirt or pebbles from near your ancestors' headstones and place it on your White Table. The deeper your research and the more serious your commitment to learning about your ancestry, the greater your connection to your roots will be. By gaining a sense of the places where your family developed, you will gain a sense of the place you live. Instead of being a rootless tourist wandering through a landscape of shopping malls and office buildings, you will become a part of the land itself—or will be encouraged to move to a place where you can not only live but *belong*.

You may not know your blood ancestry if you were adopted. In that case you should pay tribute to the people who raised you; they were instrumental in shaping your character and making you the person that you are today. (Even if you know your parents, you should not hesitate to honor a beloved teacher, a foster parent, a family friend, or someone else who touched your life and passed on. There is more to ancestry than blood. Providing the genetic material for a new life is important, but so is providing that new life with guidance and support.)

You should also pay tribute to your ethnic ancestors. Learn something about the culture from whence your biological family came, particularly the rites by which that culture honors its dead. You may benefit from learning the language, or at least enough so that you can speak to your ancestors in their own tongue. You should also include some appropriate cultural items on your White Table. This may make some readers uncomfortable. Ethnic identity has been misused by many politicians for their own ends. They have conflated respect for one's ancestry with hatred for those who do not share that heritage, or used historical atrocities to justify contemporary ones. But you can honor your Serbian forebears without hating Bosnians; you can pay tribute to your Cambodian ancestors without burning down your local VFW as "revenge" for the Vietnam conflict.

You can find precedence for this approach in Vodou. In Africa there were regular conflicts between neighboring ethnic and linguistic groups. Yet in Saint-Domingue their customs were joined together to form the *reglaman* (structure and protocols of a Vodou ceremony). In Africa, Yoruba-speaking and Fon-speaking kings might wage war with each other. But during a Vodou ceremony, Ogou (a Yoruba spirit) is honored alongside Fon lwa such as Damballah. If you preach hatred or division in the name of your ancestors, you only dishonor them. Not only do you bring shame to their memory but you may also keep them from advancing toward a higher plane. If you stir up deceased spirits with memories of old conflicts, you only encourage them to continue in the errors they committed during life.

As your ancestral connection deepens, you are likely to see greater success in material affairs. When your ancestors take notice of you, they will do their best to see that you can finish the tasks they started—and they know that this will require money. When you are following the path for which you were born, you have the force of generations behind you. Their counsel and intervention will go a long way toward bringing you the prosperity that you, and they, need.

Afterword

Losing and making money are not moral issues so long as you are being honest. You may have a lot less money as this year ends than you did two years ago. But you are just as good or bad a person as you were then. It is a myth that money determines who you are.

BEN STEIN, THE NEW YORK TIMES[1]

AN OLD *TWILIGHT ZONE* episode, "The Rip VanWinkle Caper," features a gang of criminals who awoke from a century of suspended animation with one million dollars worth of gold bars stolen in a heist. Murderous bickering breaks out between them. Finally, the last survivor perishes of dehydration and exposure after walking a long distance through Death Valley carrying his heavy load. At the end we get the typical *Twilight Zone* kicker: one hundred years later, their "treasure" is worthless since gold had become as common as aluminum.

Food has inherent value: if you are hungry you can eat it. Water has inherent value: if you are thirsty, you can drink it. Money has only the value we assign to it. Save for the pictures and numbers, there is no real difference between a one-dollar bill and a one-hundred-dollar bill. Both are equally worthless unless you can find someone willing to offer you goods or services in exchange for those pieces of paper.

Throughout this book we have discussed how magic is not a genie in a bottle that will solve all your troubles. Rather, it is a tool, something to be used in combination with hard work and common sense to better yourself. The same could be said of money. Many people expect magic spells to cure everything that's wrong in their lives; even more people assume that the solution to all of their troubles is cash and lots of it.

In 1943 psychologist Abraham Maslow created his famous Hierarchy of Needs, an ascending list of five levels of needs that must be met one at a time: until those on a lower level are met, the ones above will go unfulfilled. The five levels of needs include, in successive order: physiological, safety, love and belonging (social), esteem, and self-actualization. Money is unquestionably useful in meeting *physiological needs* for food and shelter; it is vital for meeting *safety needs* like living in a safe area and having financial reserves to get you through an emergency. It is less helpful in filling our *social needs* for love and friendship. Although many people give it preeminent importance in meeting their *esteem needs* for status and recognition, it is almost useless in meeting our *self-actualization needs* such as truth, justice, and a search for meaning in our lives.

With money you can provide your children with a better education. But there is no guarantee that, despite the money, they won't follow the example of notorious socialite Paris Hilton, who attended (and dropped out of) several of America's most exclusive prep schools. Financial problems may be putting an enormous strain on your marriage. But once they are resolved, you may find the tensions that manifested as money arguments are now returning in a new form. Wealth does not make families happy, nor will it make you a more likable person. Wealth will neither ruin the virtuous nor redeem the corrupt; it may gain the attentions of leeches, sycophants, and gold-diggers but will be less useful in winning true love and friendship.

This is not to minimize the importance of financial success. There are definitely things that money can't buy—but it will be difficult to enjoy them until you have the money to meet your basic material needs. By using the spells and advice presented in this book, you may become more prosperous; but whether or not you become happier is up to you. Freedom from debt and poverty is not an end in itself, but the first step on a long journey. Where you go from here depends on the choices you make.

May God, the ancestors, and the lwa look after and protect us both.

Resources

Books

Vodou

If you want to learn more about the practice of Vodou in Haiti and the United States, you may find the following to be useful guides:

Divine Horsemen by Maya Deren (Kingston, N.Y.: McPherson, 1983).

The Faces of the Gods: Vodou and Roman Catholicism in Haiti by Leslie Desmangles (Chapel Hill, N.C.: University of North Carolina Press, 1992).

Haiti, History and the Gods by Colin Dayan (Berkeley: University of California Press, 1998).

The Haitian Vodou Handbook by Kenaz Filan (Rochester, Vt.: Destiny Books, 2006).

Haitian Vodou: Spirit, Myth, and Reality by Patrick Bellegarde-Smith and Claudine Michel, eds. (Bloomington, Ind.: Indiana University Press, 2006).

Mama Lola: A Vodou Priestess in Brooklyn by Karen McCarthy Brown (Berkeley, Calif.: University of California Press, 2001).

Sacred Arts of Haitian Vodou by Donald J. Cosentino (Los Angeles: University of California Press/Fowler Museum of Cultural History, 1995).

Secrets of Vodou by Milo Rigaud (San Francisco: City Lights Press, 2001).

Voodoo in Haiti by Alfred Métraux (New York: Pantheon Books, 1989).

Vodou: Visions and Voices of Haiti by Phyllis Galembo (Berkeley, Calif.: Ten Speed Press, 2005).

History and Culture

Haitian Vodou and Haitian culture are inextricably entwined. To understand one requires study of the other.

Avengers of the New World: The Story of the Haitian Revolution by Laurent Dubois (Cambridge, Mass.: Belknap Press, 2004).

From Dessalines to Duvalier: Race, Colour and National Independence in Haiti by David Nicholls (Piscataway, N.J.: Rutgers University Press, 1995).

Paradise Lost: Haiti's Tumultuous Journey from Pearl of the Caribbean to Third World Hotspot by Phillipe Girard (New York: Palgrave Macmillan, 2005).

The Rainy Season: Haiti since Duvalier by Amy Wilentz (New York: Simon & Schuster, 1990).

Taking Haiti: Military Occupation and the Culture of U.S. Imperialism, 1915–1940 by Mary Renda (Chapel Hill, N.C.: University of North Carolina Press, 2000).

An Unbroken Agony: Haiti, from Revolution to the Kidnapping of a President by Randall Robinson (New York: Basic Civitas Books, 2008).

The Uses of Haiti (3rd ed.) by Paul Farmer (Monroe, Maine: Common Courage Press, 2005).

Written in Blood, Newly Revised Edition: The Story of the Haitian People 1492–1995 by Nancy Heinl (Lanham, Md.: University Press of America, 2005).

Music

Drums are an integral part of any public Haitian ceremony: there are particular rhythms and songs used to call down the lwa, to welcome them, and to send them on their way. These compilations will give you a taste of that music.

Angels in the Mirror: Vodou Music of Haiti (Ellipsis Arts, 1997).

Caribbean Revels: Haitian Rara and Dominican Gaga (Smithsonian Folkways, 1992).

Haitian Voodoo: 101 Nations (Budamusique, 2005).

Peasant Music from Haiti (Budamusique, 1997).

Rhythms of Rapture: Sacred Musics of Haitian Vodou (Smithsonian Folkways, 1995).

Rough Guide to the Music of Haiti (World Music Network, 2002).

Voodoo: Ritual Possession of the Dead (Enterra, 1997).

Voyager Series: Voodoo Drums (Columbia River Group Entertainment, 2000).

Websites

Like just about everything else on the Internet, online Vodou resources are a mixed bag. There are many sites dedicated to "Unfailing Powerful Voodoo Magic Love Spells" and Vodou Initiation Tours; there are others that seek to warn you about the evils of Vodou and other forms of "Satanism" and bring you to Protestant Evangelicalism. But there are also a few solid web pages dedicated to Haitian Vodou and Haitian culture.

Gade Nou Leve Society
www.ezilikonnen.com

Haitian Vodoun Culture
www.geocities.com/athens/Delphi/5319/

The History of the Republic of Haiti, Haiti Archives
www.hartford-hwp.com/archives/43a/index.html

New Orleans Mistic
www.neworleansmistic.com

Sosyete du Marche
www.sosyetedumarche.com

The Temple of Yehwe
www.vodou.org

Tristatevodou Discussion List
http://groups.yahoo.com/group/Tristatevodou

La Troupe Makandal
www.makandal.org

Notes

Preface

1. Jacqueline Charles, "Smugglers, Poverty Fuel Haiti Exodus," *The Miami Herald,* July 8, 2007, www.mcclatchydc.com/world/v-print/story/17941. html (accessed August 19, 2009).

2. Jean-Jacques Rousseau, "On the Origin of Inequality: The Second Part" (1754), www.constitution.org/jjr/ineq_04.htm (accessed August 1, 2009).

3. Henry David Thoreau, "Chapter 18: Conclusion" In *Walden* (1854), http://thoreau.eserver.org/walden18.html (accessed August 1, 2009).

4. "The Isle of Wight Festival 1968–1970," www.ukrockfestivals.com/ iow1970menu.html (accessed August 3, 2009).

5. See Sir James George Frazer, *The Golden Bough,* chapter 5: "The Magical Control of the Weather," section 2: "The Magical Control of Rain," www .sacred-texts.com/pag/frazer/gb00502.htm (accessed August 3, 2009).

Chapter 1. Power

1. Kenneth Roth, "Escaping Justice," *The New York Times,* September 25, 1994, http://query.nytimes.com/gst/fullpage.html?res=9E07E5DF133A F936A1575AC0A962958260&sec=&spon=&pagewanted=all (accessed July 29, 2009).

2. Haiku by Manes Pierre, "Behind the Mountains," July 28, 2005, www .authorsden.com/visit/viewPoetry.asp?id=142223 (accessed July 29, 2009).

3. Manes Pierre, "Children's Stories and Children's Book from Haiti," Aug. 19, 2004, www.authorsden.com/visit/viewblog.asp?authorid =22622&m=8&y=2004 (accessed December 21, 2009).

4. "Haitian Proverbs," www.haitianproverbs.com (2004).

5. Jenny Gibbons, "Recent Developments in the Study of the Great European Witch Hunt," *PanGaia* 21 (Autumn 1999): 24–34.

Chapter 2. Entitlement

1. Ed Frauenheim, "Myth of Class Mobility?" at cNet News Blog, May 20, 2005, http://news.cnet.com/8300-10784_3-7-3.html?authorId=9702251 (accessed September 3, 2009).

2. Michale Sheckelford, "Haiti's Dirty Little Secret: The Problem of Child Slavery," September 12, 2006, Council on Hemispheric Affairs, www .coha.org/2006/09/haiti%E2%80%99s-dirty-little-secret-the-problem-of-child-slavery/ (accessed August 3, 2009).

3. "Haiti" at Central Intelligence Agency World Factbook (December 4, 2008), https://www.cia.gov/library/publications/the-world-factbook/geos/ ha.html (accessed December 17, 2008).

4. Heather Anderson, "In Major Shift, Americans Consider Debt an Entitlement, Manning Says," November 19, 2008, Credit Union Times, www.cutimes.com/Issues/2008/November%2019,%202008/Pages/ In-Major-Shift,-Americans-Consider-Debt-an-Entitlement,-Manning-Says.aspx (accessed August 3, 2009).

Chapter 3. Magic and Healing

1. David Goldman, "Consumer Spending Drops 1%," November 26, 2008, CNNMoney.com, http://money.cnn.com/2008/11/26/news/economy/ personal_income_spending/ (accessed August 3, 2009).

2. Melissa Healy, "Shopping's Dark Side: The Compulsive Buyer," *Los Angeles Times,* July 21, 2008, http://articles.latimes.com/2008/jul/21/ health/he-shopping21 (accessed August 3, 2009).

3. *Ibid.*

4. Mark F. Wright. "What Drives Alcohol Addiction?" *Visions*, Spring 2006, Wake Forest University Baptist Medical Center, www1.wfubmc.edu/arti-cles/Alcohol+addiction (accessed August 3, 2009).

5. "Tips on Caring for Elderly Relatives," *Health News* (February 1992), http://findarticles.com/p/articles/mi_m0857/is_n1_v10/ai_11971297 (accessed December 25, 2008).

Chapter 4. The Slave Trade

1. Carolyn E. Fick, *The Making of Haiti: The Saint Domingue Revolution from Below* (Knoxville, Tenn.: University of Tennessee Press, 1990), 32.

2. Dan King, "The Development of Ancient Mesopotamian Law" (December 5, 2002), Race and Ethnicity of Ancient Mesopotamia, www.gmalivuk .com/otherstuff/fall02/danking.htm (accessed August 3, 2009).

3. David A. E. Pelteret, *Slavery in Early Mediaeval England* (Rochester, N.Y.: Boydell Press, 1995), 77.

4. "History of Benin: Pre-Colonial (1600–1900)" (October 2005) at Official Website of Tourism in Benin, www.benintourism.com/en/interne. php?idrub=2&id=3 (accessed July 8, 2008).

5. Quoted in "The Story of Africa: Slavery: The Atlantic Slave Trade," BBC World Service, www.bbc.co.uk/worldservice/africa/features/ storyofafrica/9chapter4.shtml (accessed August 3, 2009).

6. "The Story of Africa: Traditional Religions: Islam and Christianity," BBC World Service, www.bbc.co.uk/worldservice/africa/features/ storyofafrica/6chapter5.shtml (accessed August 3, 2009).

7. Melissa Grainger, "4.5 The Impact of the Slave Trade; 4.5a: Demographic Impact," Peopling North America: Population Movements & Migration, www.ucalgary.ca/applied_history/tutor/migrations/four5.html (accessed August 3, 2009).

8. Tunde Obadina, "Slave Trade: a Root of Contemporary African Crisis," Africa Economic Analysis, www.afbis.com/analysis/slave.htm (accessed August 3, 2009).

9. Omowale Akintunde, "White Racism, White Supremacy, White Privilege, and the Social Construction of Race: Moving from Modernist to Postmodernist Multiculturalism," *Multicultural Education* (Winter 1999).

10. Kecia Ali, "Islam and Slavery," The Feminist Sexual Ethics Project (February 2004), www.brandeis.edu/projects/fse/Pages/islamandslavery .html (accessed August 3, 2009).

11. Eddie Becker, "Chronology of the History of Slavery: 1619 to 1789," http://innercity.org/holt/slavechron.html (accessed August 3, 2009).

12. Isabelle Whelan, "The Politics of Federal Anti-lynching Legislation in the New Deal Era" (London: Institute for the Study of the Americas, 2007), 39.

13. Robert and Nancy Heinl (revised and expanded by Michael Heinl),

Written in Blood: The Story of the Haitian People, 1492–1995 (Lanham, Md.: University Press of America, 1996), 26.

14. Greg Dunkel, "U.S. Embargoes Against Haiti—from 1806 to 2003," October 16, 2003, the International Action Center, www.iacenter.org/haiti/embargoes.htm (accessed August 3, 2009).

15. J. Damu, "Haiti Makes Its Case for Reparations, The Meter Is Running at $34 per Second," Millions for Reparations, www.millionsforreparations.com/haitireparations.html (accessed December 2, 2008).

16. Marie-José Mont-Reynaud, "The Failure of the American Occupation of Haiti, 1915–1934," March 2002, Windows on Haiti, www.windowsonhaiti.com/windowsonhaiti/am-occup.htm (accessed August 3, 2009).

17. "Restavek Fact Sheet—Haitian Child Slavery," Haitian Street Kids, http://quicksitemaker.com/members/immunenation/Restavek_Fact_Sheet.html (accessed December 2, 2008).

18. Robert W. Tracinski, "Apology for Slavery will Perpetuate Racism," the Ayn Rand Institute (July 13, 1997), www.aynrand.org/site/News2?JServSessionIdr012=28b5bmsgf2.app7a&page=NewsArticle&id=5136&news_iv_ctrl=1076 (accessed August 3, 2009).

19. Manning Marable, "Racism, Prisons, and the Future of Black America," PeaceWork (January 2001), www.peaceworkmagazine.org/pwork/1200/122k05.htm (accessed August 3, 2009).

20. Julia Preston, "After Iowa Raid, Immigrants Fuel Labor Inquiries," *The New York Times*, July 27, 2008, www.nytimes.com/2008/07/27/us/27immig.html (accessed August 3, 2009).

21. See www.killercoke.org (accessed August 3, 2009).

22. Jennifer Lee, "Report Cites Labor Infractions by Wal-Mart Supplier in China" City Room section at *The New York Times,* http://cityroom.blogs.nytimes.com/2007/12/12/report-cites-labor-infractions-by-wal-mart-supplier-in-china/?hp (accessed August 3, 2009).

Chapter 5. Christianity

1. Alfred Métraux, *Voodoo in Haiti* (New York: Random House, 1989), 321.

2. Leslie G. Desmangles, *The Faces of the Gods: Vodou and Roman Catholicism in Haiti* (Chapel Hill, N.C.: University of North Carolina Press, 1992), 23–24.

3. Emma George Ross, "African Christianity in Kongo," The Metropolitan Museum of Art, Heilbrunn Timeline of Art History, www.metmuseum.org/toah/hd/acko/hd_acko.htm (accessed August 3, 2009).

4. Leslie G. Desmangles, *The Faces of the Gods: Vodou and Roman Catholicism in Haiti* (Chapel Hill, N.C.: University of North Carolina Press, 1992), 27.

5. Selwyn Ryan, "Haiti—an Event Horizon, part 3" *Trinidad and Tobago Express,* April 25, 2004, Bob Corbett's Haiti Pages, www.hartford-hwp.com/archives/43a/558.html (accessed August 3, 2009).

6. Dr. David Holohan, trans., "Papa Doc's Concordat (1966)," Concordat Watch, www.concordatwatch.eu/showkb.php?org_id=847&kb_header_id=859&kb_id=1533 (accessed August 4, 2009).

7. John Kohan et al., "Things Must Change Here," *Time* magazine, March 21, 1983, www.time.com/time/magazine/article/0,9171,923360-1,00.html (accessed August 4, 2009).

8. Tom Block, "Portrait of a Folk-Hero: Father Jean-Bertrand Aristide," October 1990, Bob Corbett's Haiti Pages, www.webster.edu/~corbetre/haiti/history/recent/aristidebio.htm (accessed August 4, 2009).

9. Ibid.

10. Brendan I. Koerner. "Is Aristide Still a Priest?" *Slate,* February 17, 2004, www.slate.com/id/2095635/ (accessed August 4, 2009).

11. Larry Rohter, "Liberal Wing of Haiti's Catholic Church Resists Military," *The New York Times,* July 24, 1994.

12. Larry Rohter, "Mission to Haiti: Haiti's Priest-President Faces a Hostile Catholic Hierarchy" *The New York Times,* September 28, 1994.

13. Garry Pierre-Pierre, "Many in Haiti Are Troubled by Marriage of Aristide," *The New York Times,* January 21, 1996.

14. Howard Culbertson, "Mr. Missionary, I Have a Question (Part 4): Regional Directors, Demons, and the Dominican Republic—Some Answers by Howard Culbertson" (1987), Missions Mobilizer, http://home.snu.edu/~HCULBERT/mr3.htm (accessed August 4, 2009).

15. Erwin Fahlbusch et al., *The Encyclopedia of Christianity, vol. 2* (Grand Rapids, Mich.: Eerdmans Publishing, 2001), 497.

16. "Dr. Paul Richard Orjala (1925–2005)," December 15, 2005, Nazarene Theological Seminary News, www.nts.edu/dr-paul-richard-orjala-1925-2005 (accessed August 4, 2009).

17. David Nicholls in Leslie Bethell, *The Cambridge History of Latin America, vol. 7* (Cambridge: University Press, 1984), 570–71.

18. Janet Afary and Kevin B. Anderson, "The Seductions of Islamism: Revisiting Foucault and the Iranian Revolution," *New Politics* 10, no. 1 (Summer 2004), www.wpunj.edu/newpol/issue37/Afary37.htm (accessed August 4, 2009).

Chapter 6. Freemasonry

1. Ambrose Bierce, *The Devil's Dictionary* (1911), www.alcyone.com/max/lit/devils/ (accessed August 4, 2009).

2. Christopher Hodapp, *Freemasons for Dummies* (Hoboken, N.J.: Wiley Publishing, 2005), 85.

3. "Hamas and Freemasonry" (1988) at Grand Lodge of British Columbia and Yukon, www.freemasonry.bcy.ca/anti-masonry/hamas.html (accessed August 4, 2009).

4. "Freemasons in the French Revolution" Grand Lodge of British Columbia and Yukon, http://freemasonry.bcy.ca/texts/revolution.html (accessed August 4, 2009).

5. Mitch Abidor, trans., "Sonthonax Broadside (1793)," The L'Ouverture Project, http://thelouvertureproject.org/index.php?title=Sonthonax_Broadside_(1793) (accessed August 4, 2009).

6. Hubert Coles, "The Rise of Emperor Dessalines and the Decline of His Imperial Tyranny." In *Christophe: King of Haiti* (New York: Viking Press, 1967). See ChickenBones: A Journal for Literary and Artistic African-American Themes, www.nathanielturner.com/dessalines.htm (accessed August 4, 2009).

7. David Nicholls, *From Dessalines to Duvalier: Race, Colour and National Independence in Haiti* (New Brunswick, N.J.: Rutgers University Press, 1996), 118.

8. Personal conversation with the author.

9. Katherine Dunham, *Island Possessed* (Chicago: University of Chicago Press, 1994). Originally published New York: Doubleday, 1969.

Chapter 7. Papa Legba

1. Melville J. Herskovits and Frances S. Herskovits, *Dahomean Narrative: A Cross-Cultural Analysis* (Chicago: Northwestern University Press, 1998), 39–40.

2. Harold Courlander, *A Treasury of African Folklore: The Oral Literature, Traditions, Myths, Legends, Epics, Tales, Recollections, Wisdom, Sayings, and Humor of Africa* (New York: Marlowe & Company, 1996), 170–71.

3. Conversation with the author, August 19, 2008.

Chapter 8. Damballah

1. Wilfred D. Hambly and Berthold Laufer, *Serpent Worship in Africa* (Whitefish, Mont.: Kessinger Publishing, 2006), 14. Originally published in 1931.

2. P. Mercier, "The Fon of Dahomey." In *African Worlds,* Daryll Forde, ed. (Oxford: Oxford University Press, 1954), 220–21.

3. Jean-Claude Rage, "The Origin and Evolution of Snakes." In *Snakes: A Natural History,* Roland Bauchot, ed. (New York: Sterling Publishing, 2006), 29.

Chapter 9. Met Agwe Tawoyo

1. Marie-José Alcide Saint-Lot, *Vodou, A Sacred Theatre: The African Heritage in Haiti* (Coconut Creek, Fla.: EducaVision, 2003), 98.

2. Bob Corbett, "African-derived words in Haitian Creole" (2001), Bob Corbett's Haiti Pages, www.webster.edu/~corbetre/haiti-archive/msg07101.html (accessed August 4, 2009).

3. Bebe Pierre Louis, "Islamic Influences on Haitian Vodou," March 12, 2001, Bob Corbett's Haiti Pages, www.webster.edu/~corbetre/haiti/voodoo/islam.htm (accessed August 4, 2009).

4. Conversations with the author.

5. Quoted in Laurence A. Breiner, *An Introduction to West Indian Poetry* (Cambridge, U.K.: Cambridge University Press, 1998), 29.

6. Kenneth Chang, "Conch Shell As a Model for Tougher Ceramics," *The New York Times,* July 11, 2000, http://query.nytimes.com/gst/fullpage.html?res=9E01EFD81238F932A25754C0A9669C8B63 (accessed August 4, 2009).

Chapter 10. Philomena

1. "Saint Philomena," at Catholic Tradition, www.catholictradition.org/Saints/philomena.htm (accessed August 4, 2009).

2. Mark I. Miravalle, "Present Ecclesial Status of Devotion to Saint Philomena," 2002, The Official Website of the Sanctuary of Saint Philomena, www

.philomena.us/Present Ecclesial Status-St. Philomena Nov 4.htm (accessed August 4, 2009).

3. Scott Shane, "Startup Failure Rates—The REAL Numbers," April 28, 2008, Small Business Trends, www.smallbiztrends.com/2008/04/startup-failure-rates.html/ (accessed August 4, 2009).

Chapter 11. Kouzenn Zaka

1. Bob Corbett, "Haiti: The Post-Revolutionary Period: 1804–20," 1999, Bob Corbett's Haiti Pages, www.webster.edu/~corbetre/haiti/history/earlyhaiti/postrev.htm (accessed August 4, 2009).

2. UPI. "Haiti Census Shows High Unemployment, AIDS," May 12, 2006, Haiti Info, www.haiti-info.com/spip.php?article4382 (accessed August 4, 2009).

Chapter 12. Ogou

1. Donald J. Cosentino, "Repossession: Ogun in Folklore and Literature," In *Africa's Ogun: Old World and New, Second, Expanded Edition"* Sandra T. Barnes, ed. (Bloomington, Ind.: Indiana University Press, 1997), 303.

2. Ibid., 299–300.

3. Quoted in Randy P. Conner, David Sparks, *Queering Creole Social Traditions: Lesbian, Gay, Bisexual, and Transgender Participation in African-inspired Traditions in the Americas* (Binghamton, N.Y.: Haworth Press, 2004), 61.

4. Ibid., 62.

Chapter 13. Danto

1. Karen McCarthy Brown, *Mama Lola: A Vodou Priestess in Brooklyn, Updated and Expanded Edition* (Berkeley: University of California Press, 2001), 213.

Chapter 15. The Ancestors

1. Dana Hinders, "Divorce Statistics," LoveToKnow, http://divorce.lovetoknow.com/Divorce_Statistics (accessed August 4, 2009).

Afterword

1. Ben Stein, "They Told Me That Madoff Never Lost Money," *The New York Times,* Business Section, December 26, 2008, www.nytimes.com/2008/12/28/business/28every.html (accessed August 4, 2009).

Glossary

asogwe, houngan asogwe, mambo asogwe: Senior priest or priestess; highest rank in Haitian Vodou.

asson: A sacred rattle wielded by houngans and mambos.

Bondye: God (from the French Bon Dieu).

djevo: The room in which candidates are secluded during the kanzo ceremony.

dwapo: Decorated and sequined flags used in Vodou ceremonies.

fet: A Vodou ceremony, from the French féte (festival, party).

Florida Water: a sharp, citrus-scented cologne offered to Ogou, Danto, and other "hot" or energetic spirits.

Gineh: Literally ancestral Africa: in Vodou mythology it has become the underwater home of the lwa and the ancestors.

houngan: A priest of Haitian Vodou.

iluminasyon: A ceremony used to seek guidance in a dream.

kanzo: The ceremony of initiation as a hounsi kanzo, mambo/houngan sipwen, or houngan/mambo asogwe.

lave tet: Literally "head washing"; a ceremony that can cleanse negativity and serve as an introduction to a société.

lwa: The spirits of Haitian Vodou, also called **les anges** (the angels) or **les mistés** (the mysteries)

mambo: A female priestess of Haitian Vodou.

peristyle: A Vodou temple. (Also called a **houmfour**)

Petwo nachon: Fierce but protective spirits served with pepper, gunpowder, and whip cracks.

Pompeia Lotion: a sweet-smelling perfume made by French company L.T. Piver. Offered to "white lwa" like Damballah, Agwe, and Freda.

pwens: Magical objects or "points" that concentrate spiritual energy.

Rada nachon: The name Rada comes from "Arara," a slave port in modern-day Benin. The Rada nachon consists of popular spirits like Legba, Damballah, and Freda. Rada lwa are generally considered "cooler" and more benevolent than the hot-tempered Petwo lwa.

sipwen, houngan sipwen, mambo sipwen: The second grade of Vodou initiation.

Société: A society of Vodouisants; typically led by a houngan and mambo.

vévé: A ceremonial drawing used to symbolize and to call upon a lwa.

Vodouisants: People who practice Vodou. (Also known as **serviteurs lwa** or servants of the lwa.)

wanga: The act of performing magic ("doing wanga") or a specific magical operation.

Index